HELICOPTERS

MODERN AIR POWER

HELICOPTERS

Michael Heatley

GALLERY BOOKS
An imprint of W.H. Smith Publishers Inc.
112 Madison Avenue
New York, New York 10016

Published by Gallery Books
A Division of W H Smith Publishers Inc.
112 Madison Avenue
New York, New York 10016

Produced by
Brompton Books Corp.
15 Sherwood Place
Greenwich, CT 06830

ISBN 0-8317-6059-1

Printed in Hong Kong

10 9 8 7 6 5 4 3 2 1

PAGE ONE, LEFT: The impressive nose armament of the Soviet Union's Mil Mi-24 Hind.

PAGE ONE, RIGHT: The McDonnell Douglas AH-64A Apache displays its maneuverability.

PAGE ONE, BELOW: SA330 Puma transports of the French Army.

PAGE TWO, TOP: The US Navy's multi-purpose Seahawk variant of Sikorsky's S-70 Blackhawk.

PAGE TWO, BOTTOM: A very specialized helicopter indeed, the Mil Mi-10 flying crane.

PAGE THREE: Pictured on test, this Westland Lynx carries TOW anti-tank weapons.

THIS PAGE: Vietnam was the conflict in which the helicopter, and particularly the Bell UH-1 (pictured) really proved its worth.

CONTENTS

When the US Navy adopted the Sikorsky S-70 as its new LAMPS (Light Airborne Multi Purpose System) helicopter in September 1977, it was writing the first line of a new page in the development of the helicopter as a weapon of war. True, Sikorsky had been supplying rotorcraft to the US Armed Forces since World War II, when the R-4 opened their account in some style. The company's relationship with the Navy, too, had spanned such successful types as the S-61/H-3 Sea King, in its day the most effective submarine-hunting helicopter in the world.

· What made the S-70 noteworthy in its adoption by the Navy as the SH-60 Seahawk was that Sikorsky, despite designing and building the airframe, were not in fact the project's prime contractors. In the production LAMPS Mark III version, this honor was accorded the computer manufacturers IBM through their Federal Systems Division. With IBM responsible for the integration and total performance of the whole, Sikorsky's function was to produce an airframe to fulfill Navy performance requirements — no more, no less. The significance of this is not hard to divine. The weapons systems of the seventies and eighties had, it seemed, become so sophisticated that the airframes in which they were borne aloft were now of mere secondary importance. This was all a far cry indeed from the early years, when it had been hard to envisage a role for rotary-wing aircraft in modern warfare.

Every conflict from 1945 onwards has seen helicopters involved to a greater or lesser degree. In Korea, they had been more or less confined to casualty evacuation, while Suez saw them take an active role in tactical troop deployment. By the sixties, the nature of the Vietnam war had encouraged their development as fighting vehicles of the sky. In the Middle East, in the Falklands, in Afghanistan, the helicopter has proved an invaluable component of the modern order of battle.

It had taken a long time for the helicopter to be accepted as a weapon of warfare — and when one looks back on the types developed in the interwar years, mainly in Germany, it is not hard to understand why. Five decades later, of course, all is different: but the best place to start is at the beginning.

The helicopter's major problem was always that of overcoming torque, the equal and opposite force exerted by a powered rotor that tries to spin the helicopter's fuselage in the opposite direction to that of its own rotation. It was this seemingly insurmountable problem (now most commonly solved by means of a smaller compensatory tail rotor) that led to the interim solution of the auto-giro, pioneered by the Spaniard Juan de la Cierva. With a conventional airscrew driving the aircraft, the rotary wing 'windmilled' to provide lift – a neat solution, but one that precluded hovering in anything less than a strong wind, since forward motion (or rearward airflow) was necessary to spin the rotor.

The destruction of Irishman Louis Brennan's 1925 rotorcraft with propellers at the blade tips and a swiveling anti-torque bearing ended British interest in rotorcraft development in the interwar years. Elsewhere, however, d'Ascanio in Italy was setting the first helicopter height, distance and endurance records in 1930, broken in 1935 by the Breguet-Dorand Gyroplan Laboratoire. Neither machine, however, looked sturdy enough to have any military application —

CHAPTER ONE

The First Generation

and, as ever, all eyes turned towards Germany.

Interwar Germany was at the forefront of aviation development in almost every field. Rotorcraft was no exception, with Heinrich Focke — one of the founders of the famous Focke Wulf fighter manufacturing concern — breaking away to dedicate himself totally to rotary-wing development. Based on the fuselage of the tried and tested Fw 44 Stieglitz biplane trainer, his Fw 61 first flew in June 1936 and soon paved the way for larger, more capable machines.

Focke overcame the problem of torque by utilizing two outrigger rotors, rotating in opposite directions. These could also be used to provide directional control, being played one against the other by the use of differential/collective pitch control. After establishing a speed record of 76mph in the year after its first flight, the type graphically proved its maneuverability by being flown within a giant sports hall in Berlin before giving way

OPPOSITE: A Westland Wasp descends on to the flight deck of a Royal Navy Frigate demonstrating its unique castoring undercarriage.

LEFT: Igor Sikorsky at the controls of his historic VS-300 on the occasion of its first flight in 1939. The type, with its single main rotor/auxiliary tail rotor configuration, was the model for many thousands of helicopters to come.

to its successor. The Focke Fw 223 Drache distinguished itself as the world's first production helicopter . . . even though the actual run was limited to a total of some 20 machines. Its side-by-side rotors – mounted, like those of its predecessor, on tubular outriggers – were driven by a single 1000hp BMW radial engine, and such was its performance that a production example established a helicopter height record of 23,294 feet in 1940.

The Drache was not the only helicopter to enter German service during the war years. Anton Flettner's Fl 282 Kolibri was an altogether neater and more advanced machine that was used for shipboard reconnaissance and convoy escort duties by the German Navy from 1942, impressing all with its revolutionary design. Changes in the pitch of the intermeshing twin main rotors automatically controlled engine revolutions, while engine failure resulted in automatic feathering for autorotation. This facility permitted a controlled descent as the powerless rotor blade 'windmilled' to provide residual lift.

Although clearly inferior to the helicopter in terms of military application, the autogiro survived to see out the war years. Cierva's series of autogiros had seen limited service as observation machines, while instances are recorded of rudimentary unpowered Focke Achgelis autogiros being towed as reconnaissance platforms by German surface vessels or submarines. Several examples of these were evaluated by the US Army after the war – but, as in the civilian world, the autogiro in general was to remain eclipsed by the true helicopter due to its inability to hover unassisted and relative lack of payload.

Germany may have been setting the lead –

but Soviet expatriate Igor Sikorsky, resident in America since the Russian Revolution, wasn't going to let his adopted country down. And 50 years after the first flight of his VS-300 in 1939, helicopters bearing his name still form the backbone of the US forces' rotary-wing fleets. After experimenting with and discarding a number of main/auxiliary rotor combinations, the VS-300 was standardized with a single vertical plane tail rotor. The XR-4 pre-production model was powered by a 165hp Warner R-300 engine and, after its first flight in January 1942, was flown to Wright Field, Ohio, to become the US Army Air Force's first helicopter. The XR-4's delivery flight was itself a record achievement: pilot Les Morris flew the machine from Stamford, Connecticut to Wright Field, Ohio, in 16 hours and ten minutes of actual flying time, between 13-18 May 1942. The distance, 761 miles, was accomplished with 16 intermediate stops.

The R-4, as the service version of the VS-300 was known, notched up many more firsts, including the first helicopter landing on a carrier deck (on USS *Bunker Hill* on 6 May 1943) and the first rescue of airmen from behind enemy lines (April 1944 in the Far East while serving with the US 1st Air Commando). The type's simple layout – a single main rotor with a smaller one at the tail to counteract engine torque – became the accepted pattern. The R-4 also became Britain's first military production helicopter; it was delivered to the Royal Air Force and Fleet Air Arm, who were already interested in its anti-submarine potential.

The R-4's design had been the result of no fewer than 18 rebuilds, leading to an unattractive and aerodynamically inefficient

appearance. Sikorsky transplanted the rotor and transmission systems to a new fuselage, resulting in the R-6. The main visual identifying feature was a semi-monocoque covered tailboom, while a more stable undercarriage with an additional wheel at the nose to cope with rough-field landings completed the package. The power plant was a 240hp Franklin engine. Though the type was quickly overtaken by Sikorsky's all-new R-5, it was the first example of the constant refinement that was to typify the company's development . . . and, indeed, rotorcraft in general.

Although Korea made history as the first jet-versus-jet war, the role of the rotorcraft was strictly a supporting one, despite the indelible image reinforced by thousands of television reruns of the Bell H-13 ferrying injured troops to field hospitals beyond enemy artillery range. This vitally important though unglamorous task was also carried out by the larger, more capable Sikorsky H-5, likewise equipped with panniers outside the fuselage. Korea's main rotary-wing participants were the H-5, Bell H-13 and Hiller H-23. These were later assisted by the Piasecki HUP-1 series of heavy lifters that presaged the later Boeing Vertol Chinook tandem rotors and were primarily used for ship-to-shore operations.

The H-13 (HTL-4 to the Marine Corps) was better known in civilian life by its makers' designation, the Bell 47. Remaining in production for a quarter of a century, it proved a reliable and popular workhorse. Its Plexiglass cockpit, shaped like a bubble, provided an unparalleled field of vision, making it an ideal training or observation type. It also set a pattern for Bell helicopters in having a two-

ABOVE: First flown in 1943, the R-4 was Sikorsky's first production helicopter – the first of a long and successful line of rotorcraft to serve the US armed forces and air arms overseas.

RIGHT: Bell's Model 47 became one of the best-known and most widely used rotorcraft in history, its Plexiglass 'goldfish-bowl' cockpit befitting it for the observation role. This is a license-built example manufactured by Westland for Britain's Army Air Corps.

bladed rotor with a stabilizing system unique to the company: a common hinge for both blades left the rotor free to flap like a see-saw, while a bar with weights at each end mounted at right angles to it tended to maintain the rotor's horizontal position irrespective of the angle of the mast.

In Korea, the H-13 performed yeoman service, transporting over 8500 casualties from front line to mobile hospitals in 1951 alone. Post-Korean opportunities included large orders from the US Navy of the developed Bell 47J Ranger (a four-seater with covered tail boom): the service adopted it as their standard training and utility type with the respective designations of HTL-7 and HUL-1. Production continued until 1962, when Kawasaki, Westland and Agusta continued to bring total production to the 6000 mark. All three companies supplied the type to their respective armed forces.

The Hiller H-23 was very similar in appearance to the Bell 47/H-13, right down to its bubble cockpit and skid landing gear. Differences included a stick-like covered tail boom and a unique control system known as Rotor-Matic, involving small paddles mounted at right angles to the rotor blades. With accommodation for three persons like the H-13, it was again primarily a training and observation machine.

LEFT: One of many interesting and unusual experimental devices commissioned by the US Armed Forces was the Hiller Flying Platform, intended as an ultra-cheap airborne observation post.

BELOW: The tandem-rotor configuration was pursued by Piasecki and their successors Boeing Vertol in a line of successful military transport helicopters. The HUP Retriever, from the former manufacturer, saw US Navy service from the early 1950s.

ABOVE: A Hiller OH-23 Raven in flight above the US Army helicopter school at Fort Rucker, Alabama. Along with the Hughes OH-55, the three-seat Hiller was one of the most widely used US training helicopters.

RIGHT: A US Army Bell H-13 (as the Model 47 was termed) adds its observational ability to the firepower of a column of tanks during Exercise Long Horn in 1952. The H-13 more than proved its worth in Korea on observation and casevac duties.

ABOVE: The Lockheed XH-51, one of the first attempts to harness the rigid rotor in preference to the all-flapping, all-hinged conventional rotor. Two test machines are pictured. The type never saw service, but paved the way for the AH-56A Cheyenne.

LEFT: Sikorsky adopted a conservative policy of bringing in new ideas in parallel with existing product. The S-51 was developed from the experimental R-5 and ended up replacing the R-4 in US Army service as the H-5. Korea gave the 4-passenger type the opportunity to impress as a casualty evacuation helicopter.

Designated S-51 in civilian life, the Sikorsky H-5 had been developed in parallel with the R-4 design, and proved the next step for Sikorsky in preference to the R-6, which had taken the earlier design as far as it could go. Its first flight in October 1943 had, in fact, preceded the R-6 by some two months. Comparatively few were built – some 220 by the parent company as opposed to some 2000 H-23s and many more Bell H-13s – but with a longer fuselage holding a pilot and four passengers, and a 450hp Pratt & Whitney R-985 engine which represented a significant advance in power. In Britain, Westland built 165 examples as the Dragonfly, which served the Fleet Air Arm for many years and established a link between the two companies that was to endure into the nineties.

The H-5 distinguished itself in Korea, pointing a definite way forward for the helicopter in the service of the US Air Force's Third Air Rescue Squadron and the US Navy's Helicopter Unit 1. By the end of the war, 254 United Nations airmen had been recovered from behind enemy lines, perhaps the most notable of these rescue missions being carried out by Lieutenant David Daniels who flew his H-5 90 miles to pick up a pilot on 10 October 1950.

Korea also taught the military tacticians that if the helicopter could reach behind enemy lines to rescue wounded or downed personnel then it could equally airlift men and *matériel* to where these were most needed. Attacks could thus be mounted from the most unexpected quarters. The gains in retrieving aircrew and soldiers were twofold: firstly in ensuring the enemy could not obtain classified information through torture, and secondly reducing the need to retrain aircrew replacements which was both time-consuming and expensive.

The development of tandem-rotor helicopters was fostered by the belief – mistaken,

as it transpired – that, due to physical limitations on rotor size, multiple rotors were required to lift greater payloads. Piasecki were first to produce such a machine, the twin tandem-rotor XHRP-1 (HRP-1 Rescuer in its production form), and it was from this that the successful Vertol (later Boeing Vertol) family developed.

Vertol twin-rotors like the H-21 saw service in Vietnam on ship-to-shore duties, and even as the first rudimentary helicopter gunship. But heavy lifting was this configuration's forte – and though the mighty Mil Mi-26 Halo showed a single (eight-bladed) approach to the heavy lift problem three decades later, the Chinook family had long established themselves as the free world's favored heavy lifters. In ten years, the maximum all-up weight achievable by production rotary-wing helicopters was to rise from 5520 pounds (2500kg) to the Chinook's 33,070 pounds (15,000kg), a sixfold increase. The Chinook had a useful load of

TOP: This snow-bound landscape emphasizes the versatility of the helicopter, represented here by a US Army Vertol H-21. First flown in 1952, the type was a successful forerunner of the Chinook heavy lift family.

ABOVE: Refueling H-21s in Vietnam where they were pressed into service as the very first helicopter gunship by the simple expedient of mounting an armed soldier at the port side fuselage door.

more than seven tons under the power of two Lycoming turbines.

By the end of the Korean War, American military strategy had expanded to accommodate the promise inherent in rotary-wing flight. And with military forces — in the US, particularly — now in a better position to specify their needs, the following decade was to be a fruitful one for rotorcraft manufacturers.

The advent of the turbine engine boosted the pace of development still further and opened up an intriguing range of possibilities. The turbine's lower weight as compared with the piston engine could offset to some degree the greater fuel loads the turbine necessitated. Speeds were rising, too — from the 124.9mph (210kmh) of 1950 to the 211.9mph (341kmh) recorded in 1963 by the Sud Aviation Super Frelon. Production quantities had increased dramatically due to military demand, with Bell, Boeing Vertol, Hiller and Sikorsky all moving swiftly into four-figure production.

It was soon recognized that training helicopter pilots was a long and costly business, even if they switched from fixed-wing types. The skills needed for controlling cyclical and collective pitch were far removed from those of a conventional aircraft of the fixed-wing variety. Thus post-Korean use of rotorcraft by the US services consisted in the main of training types: the Hiller UH-12 (Model 360) and Hughes TH-55 (Model 300) were both adopted. Neither saw service in armed variants, though it is reckoned that the vast

majority of rotary-wing pilots to serve in Vietnam had trained on the TH-55 earlier in their careers.

In the US Army alone there were more than 5000 qualified helicopter pilots. The biggest training school at Fort Rucker, Alabama, was equipped with a staff of 150 and 200 light rotorcraft, mostly Bell, Hiller and Hughes designs. The Bell and Hiller helicopters have already been outlined: Hughes's Model 300 was adopted in 1964 as the US Army's standard primary helicopter trainer. A diminutive three-seater powered by a 180hp Lycoming engine, it resembled nothing more than a flying grasshopper — yet its forgiving qualities saw many of the US Army's helicopter pilots survive to graduate to more powerful battlefield machines.

The single and tandem-rotor configurations had established themselves as the norm for production types in the postwar period. Yet Flettner's experiments with twin intermeshing rotors in wartime Germany had proved fruitful, and the concept was taken up in the US by Charles H Kaman for a range of helicopters for the US Navy. The configuration had the not inconsiderable advantage of reducing overall dimensions — an important consideration when stowing helicopters on board ships. The design of Kaman's rotor systems was relatively simple, the only unusual consideration being the precise synchronization required of the forward-angled contra-rotating blades. Their swept area was greater than standard twin-rotor machines, increasing efficiency.

RIGHT: Mikhail Mil remains the greatest name in Soviet rotorcraft development. His design bureau had their first success in 1948 with the all-purpose Mi-1, a piston-engined four-seater which saw extensive service in both civil and military guises throughout the Warsaw Pact.

BELOW: More often seen in service uniform, the Hughes 300 was an ideal training mount. Over half the US rotary-wing pilots in Vietnam trained on the TH-55, as it was styled in US Army service.

The configuration was not used for new projects after the fifties, but still managed to prove the basis for some useful designs. The OH-43D (originally designated HOK-1) opened Kaman's account, serving in small numbers with the US Navy and Marine Corps from the fifties onwards. A load of five people, cargo, two stretchers and two seated orderlies or specialized equipment was carried courtesy of a 600hp Pratt & Whitney R-1340 piston engine.

Although less than 100 were built, the machine impressed the US Air Force – then looking for an interim LCR (Local Crash Rescue) helicopter – and in 1957 they ordered the type in land-based form as the HH-43 Huskie. One of the most distinctive rotary-wing types ever to wear US colors, its fuselage length was only 25 feet (the main rotors compensating for each other in torque terms and obviating the need for a tail rotor). Rear clam-shell doors ensured that every single inch of usable space was accessible, while further firefighting equipment was often underslung. Cabin space had been increased sharply by use of a small, light Lycoming T53 turbine yielding 825shp in derated form. This sat atop the cabin rather than intruding into it, while the derated engine gave good reserves of performance in hot and high conditions. Few US Air Force bases were without at least one Huskie, carrying a pilot and two firefighters with equipment or four stretchers and a medical attendant. Burma, Colombia, Morocco, Pakistan and Thailand also re-

ceived the type under the Military Aid Program.

Nikolai Kamov in the Soviet Union concentrated his efforts exclusively on naval shipboard types, mainly in the anti-submarine role, and details of these types will be found elsewhere. But despite his monopoly of shipboard rotary-wing types, he had to defer to Mikhail Mil as the Soviet Union's major rotorcraft manufacturer. Mil had begun his career with the multi-purpose Mi-1 (similar to the S-51/H-5), which was first flown in 1948 and selected in preference to the competing Yak-100 and twin-rotor Bratukhin designs. The Mi-1 Hare was refined constantly

BELOW: Charles Kaman's designs were almost all identifiable by their unusual intermeshing rotors. The HH-43 Huskie pictured here was deployed at most US air bases as a crash rescue helicopter: the firefighting equipment usually carried as an underslung load is pictured between the two helicopters.

LEFT: Mil's Mi-4 was substantially larger than its US rival the Sikorsky S-55 and was commissioned by Stalin, so it was said, after US rotorcraft had proved effective in Korea.

RIGHT: The 16-passenger Mi-4 in Finnish colours. Underslung loads were one way to overcome limits imposed by cabin size, further enhancing the helicopter's military value.

during its long production run, first in the USSR and then in Poland (where it was manufactured as the SM-1 and, with redesigned front fuselage, as the SM-2).

In the military transport field, Sikorsky and Mil appeared to be thinking along very much the same lines. The two designed almost identical rotorcraft in the S-55 and Mi-4, though the latter was in fact significantly larger. The S-55 first flew in November 1949, breaking with tradition in mounting its Pratt & Whitney Wasp radial of 600hp in the nose: a sloping drive shaft connected with the gearbox. By mounting the pilots up high for maximum visibility, a boxy and sizeable cabin with room for ten troops was achieved, while a large sliding door combined with a powerful winch to make the type a potential search and rescue workhorse. Compared with its predecessor, the S-51, the S-55 represented a quantum leap by Sikorsky – and they were rewarded by orders of nearly 1000 machines from the US services

alone, plus sizeable foreign interest. License production agreements were later concluded with SNCASE in France, Mitsubishi in Japan and Westland in Britain.

The H-19 saw service in Korea, where it was operated by the USAF's Air Rescue Squadrons from March 1951. Engine access via nose clamshell doors shortened maintenance times, while the type's versatility saw it earn further orders from the Army, Navy and Marine Corps. Almost every military role conceived for rotorcraft was carried out by the H-19 in its three decades of US service, while foreign examples flew on into the '90's.

The Mi-4 progressed from design to flight testing in seven months once Stalin had learned of the US success with rotorcraft in Korea. Code-named Hound by NATO, it first flew in 1952 and was to serve in many different roles from its entry to Soviet service the following year, these ranging from transport to interim gunship to anti-submarine stop-gap (prior to the introduction of

ABOVE: A Mitsubishi-built example of the Sikorsky S-55 in Japanese service. Its 10-troop/six stretcher capacity made it the backbone of US helicopter strength in the 1950s.

RIGHT: Sikorsky situated the S-55's power plant in the nose to save cabin space, an 800hp Wright Cyclone in production models replacing the earlier 600hp P&W R-1340.

RIGHT: Sikorsky podded a pair of Pratt & Whitney R-2800 piston engines, each of 2100hp, to provide the H-37 Mojave with a straight-through cargo/cabin area, access to which was through large nose clamshell doors.

LEFT: The helicopter proved its worth in Vietnam's inhospitable terrain in many varied roles. Here S-58 transports of the US Marine Corps disgorge their load of riflemen 22 miles south of Chu Lai.

tom of the nose even became an integral ramp. Up to 36 fully equipped troops or equivalent freight could be carried. The Marines showed their satisfaction by ordering 60 of them, while nearly 100 saw Army service as a follow-on order. One of the first ever purpose-built assault helicopters, the H-37 continued to be updated until replaced by the H-3 in the late sixties.

Sikorsky's larger S-58, first flown in March 1954 as a projected anti-submarine helicopter for the US Navy, was similar in size to the Mi-4 and boasted a comparably powerful engine in the 1525hp Wright Cyclone. The S-58 proved a useful general purpose transport and anti-submarine helicopter: its career in the latter sphere is covered more fully elsewhere.

The turbine engine could lay claim to being

BELOW: Re-engined with a turbine power plant, the S-55 enjoyed a license-built lease of life in Britain as the Westland Whirlwind.

BOTTOM: Westland repeated the turbine-engine formula with the Sikorsky S-58 to produce the Wessex. A Wessex Mark 5 of No. 848 Squadron is pictured in the Borneo jungle during the Indonesian confrontation.

the Mi-14 Haze). Like the S-55, it was powered by a single nose-mounted engine, with a drive shaft extending amidships to power the rotor: its 1700hp Shvetsov was, however, over twice as powerful as the production S-55's 800hp Wright. Hound boasted a useful feature its Western rival lacked: clam-shell style rear loading doors beneath the tail boom to allow small vehicles such as the 76mm anti-tank gun or, perhaps, a GAZ-69 command truck to be driven up a ramp and inside.

With a similar aim in mind, the US Marine Corps had looked for a heavy assault helicopter with provision for quick loading and unloading of troops and vehicles. Sikorsky met the requirement with a completely new design, the H-37 Mojave. With its two mighty 2100hp Pratt & Whitney R-2800 piston engines safely podded in shoulder positions and pilot/co-pilot looking down from a high-mounted cockpit similar to the S-55, the way was open to load through nose doors: the bot-

ABOVE: Westland's Wasp was small enough to give Royal Navy frigates a real anti-submarine capability, while also proving their worth in the communications role. Two homing torpedoes or other external stores could be carried in the ASW role.

RIGHT: A Gazelle or, later, coupled Gnome turboshaft gave the Wessex a good 'hot and high' performance which led to orders from Iraq, Brunei and other Middle East countries.

the single factor in turning the helicopter into a credible weapons platform. In a smaller, lighter unit, it offered greater power-to-weight ratio, the possibility of twin-engined safety on operations, a greater useful load and the possibility of carrying the most up to date avionics — whatever their weight.

Nowhere was this more apparent than in the case of the S-58. While the US Navy had enough confidence in Sikorsky to place pre-production orders, performance with the Wright Cyclone had failed to live up to specifications. When Westland in Britain took out a license to produce the S-58 in 1956 as the Wessex, they decided to re-engine it with a Napier Gazelle shaft turbine — and that stroke of genius transformed the type's fortunes immediately.

The first production Wessex boasted a Bristol Siddeley Gnome shaft turbine, extending range from the S-55's original 247 miles to 478 miles. And while the US Navy

had utilized the piston-engined S-55 in sub-hunting pairs of hunters (with sonar) and killers (with torpedoes), the increased payload and range combination enabled the Wessex to combine the tasks in one airframe.

Wessex deliveries to the Royal Navy started in 1960, initial production machines bearing the designation HAS (Helicopter, Anti Submarine) Mark 1. Armament consisted of machine guns, rocket pods, torpedoes and — most importantly — Nord SS.11 air-to-surface missiles. Later machines such as the HU Mark 5 employed coupled Gnomes, adding increased safety margins for the overwater flying that comprised such a large proportion of its operational role.

The Wessex saw active service in Borneo in the early sixties, airlifting marines in and out of inhospitable territory in their fight against indigenous terrorists. Used as a troop transport, it could carry up to 16 soldiers, or some 4000 pounds of freight: the previously mentioned HU (Helicopter, Utility) Mark 5 was a simplified assault transport version developed for Royal Navy Commando assault duties and first flown in 1963. Updated continuously, the Wessex grew a distinctive dorsal radome, situated amidships aft of the rotor head in its HAS Mark 3 model, introduced to service in late 1966. This continued to serve alongside the later Sea King for some years.

Westland's first rotorcraft to see Navy service was somewhat different. The Wasp had been developed in tandem with the land-based Scout, both deriving from the private venture Saunders-Roe P.531 first flown in July 1958. Westland had taken the project under its wing while absorbing both that company and Bristol's rotorcraft division in 1960. The power plant common to both was the Bristol Siddeley Nimbus, though P.531 prototypes had initially relied on the French Turboméca Turmo. The two were identical in overall dimensions, but after evaluation the Royal Navy demanded detail changes to the Wasp which included a castoring-wheel undercarriage, a hinged tail boom and an uprated version of the Nimbus developing 710shp (as opposed to the Scout's 685shp).

The Wasp's diminutive size permitted operation from platforms mounted at the stern of frigates of the *Tribal* and *Leander* classes. Two underslung homing torpedoes gave an anti-submarine capability, although the type was most often used for fleet communications work. Its hardiness in operation made it an ideal companion for surveys in the South Atlantic, while Brazil, the Netherlands, South Africa and New Zealand all also operated the type.

Back on land, the Scout also performed communications duties before getting in at the front end of the anti-tank revolution. The

LEFT: Developed from the P.531 project initiated by Saunders-Roe in the mid-1950s, the Scout differed from the Wasp. It had a less powerful engine and simplified skid landing gear.

BELOW: Although more usually seen with torpedoes in the anti-submarine role, the Wessex could also mount rocket pods and machine guns, and is seen here with air to air missiles.

addition of air-to-ground missiles made it one of the earliest tankbusters, albeit something of an interim solution. Export orders saw it supplied to Bahrein, Jordan, Uganda and Australia. It supplanted – and then replaced – the lightweight, piston-engined Saunders-Roe Skeeter in British Army Air Corps service.

Westland's success with the turbine-engined Wessex saw them repeat the exercise with the earlier Sikorsky S-55. License-built as the Whirlwind with a Wright, Pratt & Whitney or indigenous Alvis Leonides piston engine, it also proved amenable to the installation of a Gnome turboshaft. The resulting Series 3, first flown in February 1959, became – with the Wessex – the Royal Air Force's main general-purpose rotary-wing transport. Two were operated by the Queen's Flight for VIP transport until superseded by

the Wessex, while Coastal Command's bright yellow Whirlwinds distinguished themselves for two decades in the search and rescue role around Britain's coasts.

The Whirlwind also took part in the Anglo-French Suez landings of 1956, making itself conspicuous by becoming the first helicopter to be used operationally by British armed forces. On 6 November Whirlwinds from the aircraft carriers HMS *Ocean* and *Theseus* transported 45 Royal Marine Commando ashore in the wake of a seaborne assault. With little ground fire encountered, this was accomplished with no casualties.

Agusta in Italy were to establish production lines of several tried and tested US designs in the 1960s and 1970s, but their 35-seat A101G troop carrier was an indigenous design similar in scale to the Sud Super Frelon. Designed to an Italian Air Force specification, its alternative loads included 18 stretchers and five attendants or up to 11,025 pounds of cargo.

Bell had established a world-beater in the H-13/Model 47 – and they followed it with a helicopter that was to revolutionize the face of rotary-wing warfare in Vietnam. The genesis of the design predated the sixties, however, being the winner of the US Army's design competition for a turbine-powered utility helicopter in the wake of Korea. The specification neatly plugged a gap between observation machines and the heavy lifters pioneered by Piasecki. The original UH-1, a ten-seat utility machine, made its first flight in prototype form in October 1956, with a rotor diameter of 44 feet, gross weight of 8500 pounds and a useful load of 3980 pounds. Some 10,000 production machines later, the Bell 214 had increased rotor diameter to 50 feet, nearly doubled gross weight to 16,000 pounds and could carry loads of up to 8000 pounds on an external sling. All this was achieved with power in reserve, leaving enough to maintain sea level performance to 19,685 feet (6000 meters).

ABOVE: The Whirlwind distinguished itself for many years as the chief air-sea rescue helicopter in action around the coast of Britain until replaced in the 1980s by the Sea King. A stretcher case is winched up to the open starboard door.

LEFT: The A 101G was one of the few indigenous designs to be developed by the Italian Agusta company, better known for their license manufacture of US designs. Powered by three Rolls Royce Gnomes, it had a capacity of 35.

RIGHT: Appropriately pictured in Polish service, the Mil Mi-2 turbine-powered derivative of the Mi-1 was manufactured only in Poland by WSK. Widely used as a training machine, it nevertheless saw service on the battlefield, witness this smoke-generating example.

The Soviet counterpart to the UH-1, the Mil Mi-2, was unusual in that, although designed in the USSR, it was never produced there. Manufacture was based in Poland where the state-owned PZL concern set up a production line in 1965. Since then over 5000 have been produced and delivered to a variety of military operators, as well as civil owners. The Mi-2 was developed from the piston-engined Mi-1, with a larger cabin and two Isotov turboshafts mounted atop the cabin instead of the former's single piston engine.

The type was developed so successfully by its new manufacturers that it became the Soviet Union's standard training helicopter. Although most often seen otherwise as a transport and observation helicopter (it has a capacity of a pilot and eight passengers), the Mi-2 has been seen sporting four pylon-mounted Sagger missiles in pairs on rudimentary fuselage pylons. Its NATO code-name is Hoplite.

By the late fifties, tandem-rotor heavy lift helicopters previously associated with Piasecki had been gathered together under the Boeing Vertol umbrella. As with Sikorsky's single-rotor designs, the impact of the turbine engine had been of incalculable benefit — and the chief beneficiaries were the US forces in gaining a significant heavy-lift capability in the shape of the H-46 (Navy) and CH-47 (Army).

The H-46 (manufacturer's designation Model 107) had been intended as a joint military/civilian venture. When the market for military heavy lift helicopters became obvious, Boeing Vertol devolved the responsibility for civil marketing to Kawasaki in

LEFT: Pictured in US Marine Corps colors, the Boeing Vertol H-46 Sea Knight assault transport equipped five squadrons of that service. The US Navy also operated the H-46 to supply its vessels with essential stores and ammunition.

LEFT: The CH-47 Chinook was twice as powerful as the H-46, and was consequently produced in greater numbers. Replacing three different helicopter types in US service, it was widely exported and remained in production through three decades.

Japan and concentrated on fulfilling service orders. Though the US Army evaluated the type as the YHC-1A, it was the Marine Corps that proved more interested in the type as an assault transport. Known as the Sea Knight, this derivative was styled the Model 107M (for Marine Corps) and featured rear-loading ramps as well as the obligatory folding rotor blades. Five Marine squadrons were operating the CH-46A by 1965, while the US Navy operated the type for two decades on the ship-to-shore stores, personnel and ammunition supply duties known as vertical replenishment (VERTREP).

Though Canada, Sweden and Japan all bought military examples, a developed helicopter that was twice as powerful became Boeing Vertol's tandem-rotor flagship. This was the CH-47 Chinook. Selected in March 1959 as winner of a US Army design competition to find a 'battlefield mobility' helicopter, it could carry a two-ton load internally or an amazing eight tons with the

help of an external sling. Such a capability was indeed unique, and kept the type rolling off production lines in the eighties.

With an increase in fuselage length of six feet to 51 feet and rotor diameter of nine feet to just over 59 feet, the Chinook was clearly no candidate for shipboard operation from anything less than an aircraft carrier. But its useful load now extended to take in 33 to 44 equipped troops, or 27 paratroops, or 24 stretchers and two attendants: its predecessor could accommodate just 25 troops or 15 stretchers. Two 2650shp Lycoming T55s were essential requirements for a helicopter expected to airlift any component of the Pershing missile system. And so effective did the type prove that it replaced no fewer than three of its predecessors — the H-21 Shawnee, H-37 Mojave and H-34 Choctaw. The benefits in terms of maintenance and spares commonality hardly need elaboration.

In Vietnam, the Chinook excelled itself, acting as a flying casualty ward on occasion

ABOVE: The Chinook was rare in making a success of the tandem-rotor configuration. The type seems likely to remain the mainstay of the US Army's heavy-lift rotary-wing force well into the 21st century.

in between recovering downed aircraft, airlifting refugees, and transporting troops and supplies. So effective was the Chinook, in fact, that the Royal Air Force placed orders for the type over two decades after its first flight, using it extensively in the Falklands campaign. As with the US Army, the Chinook seemed set to provide the service with a viable heavy-lift capability until well into the twenty-first century.

Few other tandem-rotor helicopters proved successful. The Westland Belvedere was developed from the single-engined Bristol Sycamore light observation helicopter which had distinguished itself as the first helicopter to be designed and built in Britain after World War II — albeit designed by Austrian exile Raoul Hafner. Despite being based on tried and tested components, the new type ran into vibration problems on its 1951 debut, resulting in an eight-month delay to first flight. The Belvedere finally entered service in 1961 to provide the RAF with a short-lived heavy lift capacity — but while large loads such as missiles, small helicopters and military vehicles could be underslung, limited cabin access and dimensions gave it a poor internal capacity of 19 troops or 12 stretcher cases. By the end of the sixties, it had been withdrawn from service — and though its intended replacement, the Chinook, was initially canceled in a change of government, the replacement originally went through several years after it was first mooted.

The Soviet Yak-24 emerged from the Yakovlev design bureau, noted for its fixed-wing products: it had only two small experimental machines to its name when development started in 1952. Alas, their 'Horse' (as it was dubbed by NATO) proved to be an unreliable beast of burden for the Soviet armed forces — indeed, its problems in many ways paralleled those of the Belvedere. Two of the four prototypes were lost during the early part of the development program, and the project never really recovered momentum after a five-month delay due to severe rotor vibration. Power was supplied by two 1750hp Shvetsov piston engines. Nevertheless, the Yak-24 — significantly, the bureau's last effort to break into the helicopter field — was the largest rotorcraft yet flown on its first flight, with a length of 70 feet, rotor diameter of 69 feet and gross weight of 35,275 pounds. As Mil was to show three decades later with its mighty Mi-26, the tandem-rotor concept was not the only way to lift ever more weighty loads — and the problems faced by the Chinook's would-be rivals tended to suggest the configuration had exhausted its useful life.

RIGHT: Despite this impressive show of strength with an underslung Whirlwind, the Westland Belvedere was among the Chinook's less successful rivals in the heavy lift field. Retired from RAF service by 1970, it was replaced by the Chinook over a decade later.

BELOW: Yakovlev's Yak-24 was another short-lived tandem-rotor heavylifter. First flown in 1952, it was then the world's largest rotorcraft, but failed to make a mark after a troubled development period.

Vietnam saw the helicopter come of age as a weapons platform and prove its versatility in the battlefield beyond all doubt. Casualty evacuation was added to the rotary-wing role in Korea, but the helicopter proved even more versatile in the long, protracted Vietnam conflict. The often impassable terrain, providing perfect cover for the unseen Vietcong enemy (who were already armed with the advantage of local knowledge), required all the flexibility the helicopter could offer. And even though President Kennedy originally committed US helicopters purely for supply purposes, this was not to remain the case for long.

When the USNS *Card* arrived in Saigon in 1961 bearing 32 Piasecki H-21 Workhorse helicopters it represented the first direct US involvement in the war. 400 men from the 8th and 57th Light Helicopter Transportation Companies accompanied the aircraft, and both men and machines were soon in action. First operations were assisted by the element of surprise, as in 'Operation Chopper', airlifting 1000 South Vietnamese paratroopers in a raid on a suspected Viet Cong headquarters ten miles from Saigon. As time passed, a regular pattern was established of units who were ferried from barracks to operational areas in the morning, to be returned by helicopter the same evening. These so-called 'Picnic Lunch' excursions were not, however, regarded as efficient use of men or machines.

The Piasecki (later Vertol) H-21 in this form won the accolade of being the first helicopter gunship, with a light machine gun mounted at the side door. This was not, however, adequate, and in these initial stages US troops were ordered not to fire unless fired upon.

It was soon evident that operations would have to become more organized and sophisticated. The US Marine Corps added their Sikorsky H-34 (S-58) Seahorses to the order of battle, and it was these that, in assisting Vietnamese troops in the Mekong Delta on 24 April 1962, retrieved one of their number brought down by small-arms fire that had ruptured an oil line. This episode brought home the helicopter's vulnerability from attack by ground fire – a problem that was never satisfactorily overcome.

The US Army quickly developed its Airmobile program, creating both Air Cavalry units and a new breed of helicopter pilots from enlisted men to overcome the problem of creating a whole new layer of pilot officers: none of the US armed forces had trained enlisted pilots since World War II. Having trained the pilots, the next requirement was for more helicopters. The manufacturers responded to the challenge, and the Vietnam period saw rotorcraft production hit new heights: Bell, for example, had subcontract work occupying almost all of the Beechcraft aeroplane manufacturing factories.

The leading type in production was the Bell HU (later UH-1). Nicknamed Huey – as its earlier designation suggested – it received the accolade of being the first turbine-powered aircraft of any kind to enter service with the US Army . . . just the first of its many distinctions. In Vietnam it also served with the Marine Corps and Navy, the latter naming them Seawolfs and operating search and destroy/rescue missions launched from LST landing vessels. First flown on 22 October 1956, the Huey entered service three years later – and from the outset it was clearly going to prove an able performer. Its capa-

CHAPTER TWO

Vietnam and After

cious cabin – the 1100hp Lycoming T53 was mounted above, leaving room for seven (later 14) troops – was accessible via large sliding doors, ideally suiting it to the casevac role carried out manfully but less effectively by its little sister the Bell 47 in the earlier Korean campaign. But as Vietnam developed, the door space was often occupied by a gun-toting GI – and it was soon decided that more permanent forms of armament would be effective. Helicopters had found themselves priority targets – their movements from base areas to forward combat zones increased as the conflict escalated, and their vulnerability to ground small-arms fire had been illustrated on several occasions. It was time for the Huey to bite back.

The US Army's response was to form the Utility Tactical Transport Helicopter Company in 1962, equipping its fleet of UH-1s with 0.3 inch machine guns and 2.75 inch rockets. The former represented a basic ability to deter, but it was the latter that

OPPOSITE: Air support from rotary-wing types proved crucial in many Vietnam actions. Here a US Marine Corps Bell AH-1J SeaCobra assists an amphibious attack on a beach, its rocket and nose gun armament clearly visible.

ABOVE: The Sikorsky
H-34, which proved an
early success in
Vietnam when it
successfully carried
out a rescue mission
behind enemy lines in
April 1962.

sowed the seeds of the gunship. Cylinder-like pods bolted on to the fuselage typically held seven rockets apiece – and, no matter how crude, this installation could be replaced in the field in a matter of minutes.

Armed and ever more capable, the Huey became the chosen mount of the US Army's Air Cavalry – a force stationed at An Khe on Route 19 who used caravans airlifted into remote areas by CH-47 heavy lifters as temporary living quarters for their aircrew. So intensive were their operations that there were frequently hundreds of helicopters in the air at any one time. Yet there were some who believed that, by basing their strategy heavily on the helicopter, the US were at a disadvantage when poor weather conditions prevented effective air support. And it is certainly true to say that the advent of the SA-7 Grail surface-to-air missile, effective against aircraft below 10,000 feet, made helicopter operations considerably more hazardous.

These criticisms notwithstanding, the Air

Cavalry more than once drew the highest praise from Army commanders whose success often owed much to support from the air. The assistance rendered to the 1st Battalion of the 7th Cavalry in the Ia Drang Valley campaign of 1965 was one such occasion, on which Lieutenant Colonel H G Moore commented that they 'ran the gauntlet time after time to help us . . . most of them took hits.' That particular three-day battle saw two UH-1s damaged severely enough to require retrieval and repair, but all others remained airborne in the face of heavy fire – a testament to the Huey's ability to absorb damage.

In the event of a serious problem, the UH-1 could be airlifted to a repair depot by a CH-47 or CH-54, the US Army's heavy lift helicopters – and more often than not would be back in action within days. Its duties were many and various, transporting personnel and supplies one minute and directing a hail of machine gun fire into the jungle the next.

The Huey was constantly upgraded by its

LEFT: The Piasecki Workhorse was the first US helicopter deployed in the Vietnam theater, when 32 arrived in Saigon in 1961 aboard the USNS *Card.* An H-21 of the 93rd Helicopter Company is pictured on operations in early 1962.

RIGHT: The UH-1 Huey proved nearly immune to heavy fire compared with other types – and even when downed could be salvaged and airlifted to a repair depot behind the lines by a CH-47 Chinook.

LEFT: An airworthy example of the UH-1, seen here in its UH-1E variant which replaced both the Kaman H-43 and the fixed-wing Cessna Bird Dog with the US Marine Corps.

BELOW: A CH-47 Chinook airlifts *matériel* into a forward area. Although its size made it vulnerable to ground fire, the type saw widespread and effective service in Southeast Asia.

BELOW RIGHT: Built with a backbone rather than a conventional fuselage, Sikorsky's S-64/CH-54 Skycrane was the ultimate in heavy lift helicopters, serving in Vietnam alongside the Chinook.

makers, frequently in response to requests and suggestions from the front line. The T53 turboshaft was uprated to 1400 shp, while the UH-1C's wide-chord 'door hinge' rotor increased both maneuverability and speed. Like most improvements, it became a standard feature. The UH-1D was the first to be accorded a new manufacturer's designation, Model 205, recognizing a 2 foot fuselage stretch which, combined with relocation of fuel storage, enabled a pilot and 14 troops to be accommodated. This represented a 100 per cent increase in passengers carried.

Still the variants continued. The UH-1E proved its versatility by replacing two types in US Marine Corps service – not only the rotary-wing Kaman H-43 but the fixed-wing Cessna O-1 Bird Dog. The UH-1N introduced an 1800hp Pratt & Whitney Aircraft of Canada PT6 coupled-turbine power plant, adding twin-engine reliability to the Huey's other features. The UH-1's final accolade came not in Vietnam but in Europe, where Agusta's sophisticated twin-engined derivative, the AB.212, was doing good business as a state-of-the-art ASW helicopter in the late eighties – over 30 years after its first flight.

Still in the sixties, the success of the armed UH-1 had led the US Army to consider a purpose-built helicopter gunship or Advanced Aerial Fire Support System (AAFSS). A fiercely contested design competition had seen Lockheed emerge victorious – somewhat unexpectedly, since their rotary-wing experience was at that point confined to the experimental rigid-rotor XH-51.

The AH-56 Cheyenne took the XH-51 several stages further, combining a rigid

four-bladed rotor with a small fixed wing to offload it in forward flight. Not only did it have a tail rotor but also a pusher propeller – an unusual feature which, like the retractable landing gear, was intended to increase speed. The result was a sleek but highly unusual rotorcraft, capable of delivering its offensive load of grenades (from a nose-mounted launcher), machine guns, rockets and anti-tank missiles at speeds of up to 240 mph.

No matter how impressive its paper performance, however, the Cheyenne was always going to be an expensive machine – and its ambitious design concepts hardly seemed suited to a war of attrition in inhospitable territory. The sophisticated AH-56's reliance on maintenance facilities would negate some of its undoubted advantages. In these circumstances, Bell's decision to develop a pared-down version of the UH-1 as a specialized gunship seemed more than sensible. The Huey's tried-and-tested engine and

ABOVE: Despite its impressive performance, Lockheed's AH-56 Cheyenne was cancelled due to its expense and complexity, the smaller, simpler HueyCobra being judged more suited to the Vietnam theater. Note the retractable undercarriage, just one of the features that conferred a 240 mph top speed.

LEFT: Father leads son . . . the UH-1 Huey (foreground) pictured with the SeaCobra, the naval variant of the AH-1 HueyCobra attack helicopter developed from the UH-1 in the light of early Vietnam operations.

ABOVE: The helicopter's traditional vulnerability to small-arms fire is all too graphically illustrated by this CH-46 Sea Knight downed during July 1966's Operation 'Hastings'. 13 troops perished as the giant rotorcraft hit the ground.

11½ inches could hold packs containing up to 76 2.75 inch rockets. Compared with its UH-1 'interim gunship' predecessor, the Huey Cobra won out on all counts, boasting faster speed to station, longer endurance and heavier firepower. Its low development cost was reflected in a very attractive unit cost, and it was this that finally killed off the Cheyenne. Within two years of first flight, the AH-1 already had orders for 530 US Army examples.

The US Marine Corps persuaded Bell to add twin-engine reliability (a must for overwater operation) to the HueyCobra's already impressive attributes, and the result was the AH-1J SeaCobra. Similar in appearance to earlier Cobras, it boasted an 1800 shp Pratt & Whitney Aircraft of Canada T400 twin turboshaft and a 28 per cent increase in power necessitated internal strengthening of the airframe due to the additional torque.

The Cobra was the subject of continual updating and improvement, culminating in the Cobra 2000. Based on the US Army's AH-1S, it boasted the civil Model 412's four-bladed rotor, an uprated Avco Lycoming engine, plus Hughes TOW 2 missiles, cannon, rockets, fire control and night vision sensors.

The creation and evolution of the helicopter gunship was one of the more valuable lessons of Vietnam. But that was not the only far-reaching result of the conflict. The US Army's order of battle in Vietnam had latterly included no fewer than seven distinct types: the Bell AH-1 gunship, the Bell UH-1 transport, medevac and command helicopter, the Hughes OH-6 for light reconnaissance, the Bell OH-58 patrol/target acquisition helicopter, the Sikorsky CH-3 aircrew recovery vehicle, the Sikorsky CH-54 heavy lifter, and the Boeing-Vertol CH-47 for troop transport and forest clearance. At the end of the day, the maintenance demands of such a wide range of types, from the mighty twin-rotor CH-47 Chinook to the tiny OH-6 'flying egg', were impossibly heavy, suggesting a combination of roles at least for the smaller helicopters mentioned. In fact, the US Army's response was the LHX specification which attempted to combine the AH-1, UH-1, OH-6 and OH-58 into one multi-purpose airframe sharing the same power plant and systems. A requirement existed for 5000–7000 of these. It was ironic that as the successful HueyCobra had sprung from specialization, so the trend was now to be reversed. And as if to confirm this, McDonnell Douglas were looking at ways for developments of the AH-64, the HueyCobra's designated successor, to fulfill these roles.

The Soviet Union's first gunship was manufactured on a somewhat different scale to the HueyCobra in their Mil Mi-24 Hind, a

mechanical systems were borrowed wholesale: both conferred reliability, while using the same spares as its forebear reduced maintenance headaches. The company was later to repeat the trick with the military JetRanger, the OH-58 Kiowa, when the Hughes OH-6 overran on costs – but when the Bell 209/AH-1 HueyCobra first flew on 7 September 1965 it already looked a winner.

The UH-1's power plant, transmission and rotor system were retained, but the slim, streamlined minimum cross-section fuselage was completely new except for the tail assembly. Pilot and gunner sat in tandem, but reversed usual practice in seating the gunner forward and slightly below his companion for maximum visibility under a long, glazed cockpit. This arrangement was to become standard in all subsequent gunship types. Two 7.62mm miniguns in a nose-mounted turret, each with six barrels, presented a formidable calling card, while the miniature stub wings with a span of 10 feet

LEFT: A 155mm howitzer poses no problem to a CH-54 Skycrane during Operation 'Crazy Horse', a typical Vietnam search-and-destroy mission. The mobility conferred by such helicopters gave the US and South Vietnamese forces a compensating advantage when faced with inhospitable terrain and an organized enemy.

BELOW: The Communist response to the lessons of Vietnam came in 1973 with the Mil Mi-24 Hind helicopter gunship. The earliest Hind-A version, distinguishable by a larger, glazed, 'greenhouse' cockpit, is pictured.

type first noted by the West in 1973. Yet the Soviet Union experimented with armed helicopters during Exercise Dnepr in 1967, the same year that the AH-1 entered service in Vietnam. The fact that their own gunship took so long to develop and its eventual size, suggested a continuing dominant belief in the helicopter's role as a troop carrier.

It is difficult to underestimate the Mi-24's impact on Soviet rotary-wing warfare. Despite several new contenders which are detailed in a later chapter, Soviet rotary-wing strength continued to depend heavily on the Mi-24. Like the HueyCobra, it built on the engines and transmission systems of an existing type, in this case the Mil Mi-8 — but in size, the type was the complete antithesis of its Western rival, its capacity for eight fully armed troops suggesting a dual role.

The Hind's firepower, however, could not be taken lightly. Guns, guided missiles and rocket pods combined in a deadly cocktail to make 1975's Hind-D a formidable fighting machine. It had also adopted the now-standard gunship configuration of a stepped, tandem cockpit. By the time Hind-E

arrived, its already capable armament included laser-designated AT-6 Spiral missiles (adding to the AT-2 wire-guided weapons already observed), UB-32 rocket pods, and a twin-barrel 23mm GShL-23 cannon mounted either side of the nose. Soviet sources claimed a kill:loss ratio of up to 19:1 for the type, over 800 of which were in service with Frontal Aviation in the mid-eighties.

The latest Hind-F variant saw the nose turret deleted and replaced by a twin-barrel cannon of 30mm caliber. Over 2300 models had been delivered by the late eighties, with Bulgaria, Czechoslovakia, East Germany, Hungary and Poland among its Warsaw Pact operators. A dozen countries outside the Pact, including Algeria, India and Vietnam, had also received it.

The deployment of the Hind in the eighties in Afghanistan illustrated once again the vulnerability of rotary-wing craft to attack from the ground. And though the Mi-24 was initially spectacularly successful against lightly defended rebels, its shortcomings were also exposed. The large engine exhausts of the Hinds were targets for the heat-

ABOVE: Conceived and developed by Hughes, the AH-64 Apache became a McDonnell Douglas project late in the 1980s after the companies merged. Destined to replace the HueyCobra, the Apache fulfilled the US Army Advanced Attack Helicopter (AAH) specification announced as far back as 1973.

seeking weaponry such as the US-supplied Stinger, now widely available, and the sight of flares being ejected to mislead such warheads was not uncommon.

In the battlefield of the future, the Hind's size would probably prevent it from operating out of ambush positions, while its lack of acceleration from a hovering position would make it vulnerable to fixed- or rotary-wing predators. Furthermore, the type's armament would be unlikely to prove effective against a more agile adversary, being optimized for air-to-ground attack. Nevertheless, the fact remains that in the Hind the Soviet forces had a helicopter feared by their adversaries. And with the advent of such battlefield superiority types as the Mi-28 Havoc and Kamov's Hokum, the issue of size and vulnerability seemed unlikely to pose such a question mark over its future.

Confirmation that the Soviet Union had digested the implications of Vietnam continued to register. During the Ethiopian War in 1978, General V I Petrov had used helicopters to airlift men, PT-76 tanks and armored personnel carriers over a range of mountains in a successful attempt to engage Somali troops in a surprise attack from the rear. The type used for this venture was the Mil Mi-6 Hook, Soviet Frontal Aviation's standard heavy-lift helicopter until the in-

LEFT: The business end of Mikhail Mil's Hind gunship, a helicopter described by military commentators on first sighting in the 1970s as 'a helicopter battle-cruiser'

BELOW: This view of the Hind in flight emphasizes its size. Unlike the US HueyCobra, which made a virtue of its minimum fuselage, Hind shows its dual role as attack helicopter and troop transport, with a cabin capacity of eight fully-armed troops.

LEFT: Mil's formidable Mi-28 Havoc demonstrates why the designers dubbed it 'the heavy one'. It is pictured in 1989, the year the Soviets revealed it to the West.

RIGHT: An RAF SA 330 Puma airlifts a 105mm light gun during exercises. Underslung loads increased the carrying capability of this medium transport which, with the Wessex, was the mainstay of the RAF's rotorcraft transport force in the 1970s and '80s.

LEFT: Mil's mighty Mi-28 Halo transport shows off its enormous eight-bladed rotor, with a 105-foot diameter. Cargo-carrying capacity was huge too, with a hold the equivalent of a fixed-wing C-130 or An-12.

troduction of the mighty Mi-26 Halo in the 1980s. The lesson of the Somalia campaign soon percolated through to Soviet forces in Europe, where a force of 400 tactical helicopters was doubled in strength in just five years. In time of war, of course, the imposing fleet operated in the colors of Russian state airline Aeroflot would be at the military's disposal, effectively multiplying their available rotary-wing transport forces severalfold.

The first British force to fuse elements of air and land combat in a cohesive whole was 24 Airmobile Brigade, declared operational in 1989. Exercises in West Germany in the same year proved that a light, air-portable force could effectively counter tanks in what is generally considered the battleground on which a conventional World War III would be fought. In the exercises, they were supported by 40 Army Air Corps Lynx helicopters, plus the transport element of 12 Pumas and 10 Chinooks loaned by the Royal Air Force — a level of assistance observers regard as un-

likely to be forthcoming in wartime.

As with US deployment of the helicopter in Vietnam, the rule book had to be rewritten when helicopters were deployed as anything other than free agents. When poor visibility, unfavorable weather or other factors precluded the use of rotary-wing craft, then the problems multiplied. In European terrain, air cover would prove crucial in rendering such missions possible.

General Sir Brian Kenny, Commander in Chief of the British Army of the Rhine, stated his belief in 1989 that the cuts in armor dictated by future arms control agreements would dictate that forces would have to be more mobile in order to cover the same ground. This pointed to the possibility of a future multi-national heliborne division supported by third-generation gunships such as the PAH-2 (see Chapter 5). Notwithstanding the climate of reduction in defense spending, the place of the helicopter in modern warfare seemed assured.

So much of the innovation stemming from the United States has been fostered and forced by the practice of design contests. The most fruitful as far as the rotary-wing world was concerned was the Light Observation Helicopter specification of 1960. No fewer than three outstanding helicopters emerged from the contest – and as always the civil spinoffs were at least as lucrative for most of the manufacturers as the military contracts.

Of the 12 companies which put forward designs to the LOH specification, Bell, Fairchild Hiller and Hughes were the trio selected to manufacture prototypes. They produced five machines apiece, and these were subjected to service scrutiny at Fort Rucker, Alabama, from late 1963 onwards. The process took fully 18 months, the winner having to meet an exacting brief that included casualty evacuation, close support, light transport and observation. The turbine used for all three of the LOH contenders was the Allison T63, a free-shaft unit designed specifically for this purpose which had a power turbine spool the size of a two liter oil can yet produced 250shp at optimum operating speed.

Hughes' OH-6A won the day and, named Cayuse, it entered Army service in 1966. But despite creating a plethora of speed, altitude and distance records – the last of which, 2213 miles (3561km) set on 6-7 April 1966 by R G Ferry, still stands today – the pleasingly streamlined type proved expensive. And with 65 per cent of the total Army requirement of 4000 still to be delivered when the design competition was reopened in 1967, there was clearly much to play for.

Bell and Fairchild Hiller had both gone on to develop their LOH designs for the lucrative civil market. The FH-1100 derived from the unsuccessful OH-5A found some success as an executive helicopter – but it was Bell's JetRanger that was to sweep the boards as the most popular light and corporate rotary-wing type since the 47. Production lines existed at Fort Worth and (license manufactured by Agusta) in Italy, so the type was a known quantity both performance and pricewise – and it was no surprise when the JetRanger donned uniform (plus a larger rotor and military avionics) to become the OH-58 Kiowa.

Deliveries began in May 1969, and within four months the type was operational in Vietnam. An initial order of some 2200 was placed, with the Canadian Armed Forces, Australia and US Navy quick to join the order book. The latter's 40 TH-57A SeaRangers were dual-control machines for operation by Naval Air Training Command at Pensacola, Florida. The Bell 406 development of the JetRanger/Kiowa was selected in 1981 as winner of the Army Helicopter Improvement Program (AHIP) to develop a scout helicopter. A MDAC/Northrop mast-mounted sight facilitated day/night viewing and communications as well as being a very obvious visual reference point. With laser rangefinder and target designators among its equipment, this was intended as an updated Kiowa (OH-58D) to scout for helicopter gunships in Europe. An armed AH-58D Warrior version was also ordered in small numbers, though most would be refurbished and modified OH-58As. Saudi Arabia ordered 15 armed variants named 'Combat Scout' with two GIAT 20mm gun pods, on either side of the fuselage. Amazingly, the FH-1100 made a comeback after several years out of production and little military interest, reappearing

CHAPTER THREE

The Second Generation

as Rogerson Hiller's RH-1100 Hornet. It debuted at the 1985 Paris Air Show, pitching to cost-conscious powers like Sri Lanka, Taiwan and Venezuela.

It was a testimony to these types' longevity that they were still being developed in the late eighties, as Third World countries sought armed helicopter capability at an affordable price. Spares commonality with widely flown civil types was also an asset, as was the tried-and-tested systems on which the designs relied.

The Hughes 500 donned warpaint once again – not as the Cayuse this time, but the Model 500M Defender. With self-sealing fuel tanks and a plethora of armament options, the type's always-attractive performance added Japan, Argentina and Israel to the order books and made up for some of the disappointment of lost US Army orders. Bell's parallel revamp of the JetRanger/Cayuse as the Texas Ranger also stirred interest, though the armaments it carried were at

OPPOSITE: Developed in parallel for the civil market as the S-61N, the capable Sikorsky SH-3 Sea King became the world's most widely used amphibious helicopter.

LEFT: Selected by the US Army in 1965 as its Light Observation helicopter, the Hughes OH-6A Cayuse performed exceptionally, but proved expensive to produce and was eventually supplanted by the Bell OH-58.

BELOW: The Hughes 500 camouflaged as the Model 500 M Defender.

ABOVE: Bell developed their rejected LOH design as the Model 206 JetRanger, one of the most successful corporate civilian helicopters ever. It was readopted by the US Army in 1968 as the Kiowa, and exported to several other nations.

least as attractive to potential purchasers as its now-venerable airframe.

'Tankbusting' helicopters were finding their way into everyone's armory, and many were merely modifications of existing types. The Sud Aviation (later Aérospatiale) Alouette, for example, had previously seen service with the French forces in the light transport, observation and communications roles. Towards the end of its useful life, it found itself in demand when its makers allied state-of-the-art weaponry with an airframe already optimized for 'hot and high' performance. The Alouette II had first flown in June 1951 and had originally been intended as an agricultural type. Broadly comparable in layout to the Bell 47, with a tubular steel tail boom and a high visibility bubble cockpit, its greatest asset was turbine power via a Turboméca Artouste (later a more powerful Astazou) turbine derated to 360shp that conferred exceptional performance at altitude. Once in uniform (initially with the

French armed forces, and later worldwide), the simple yet effective Alouette II found itself fulfilling such diverse roles as close support, battlefield reconnaissance, light transport, flying crane (a payload of over 1320 pounds was quoted), casualty evacuation (two stretchers, two sitting casualties, one attendant) and even anti-submarine warfare.

The developed Alouette III featured an enclosed tail boom and cabin: to all intents and purposes it shared little visually with the II. First flown in 1959, it could nominally carry a pilot and six passengers but enjoyed great popularity as a two-seater gunship. A quick-firing 20mm nose-mounted cannon could be supplemented with machine guns, rocket pods and wire-guided missiles. Most popular weapons in the last-named category were the manufacturers' own Aérospatiale AS 11, four of which could be carried on launcher arms that simply bolted on to the fuselage. This simple but effective philosophy was to extend

ABOVE: Aérospatiale's Alouette II, first flown in 1951 was superficially similar to the Bell 47 but had an Artouste (later Astazou) turbine power plant giving better performance, especially at altitude.

LEFT: The Alouette III followed in 1959. The pictured example carries air-to-surface missiles and a nose radar for anti-shipping duties.

the type's useful life into the 1990s.

After building some 200 Alouette IIIs under license, India's Hindustan Aeronautics developed a specialized ground attack variant, the Chetak. Standard machines found favor with over 20 air forces, including those of Jordan, Malaysia, Tunisia and Portugal, with production exceeding 1500 examples.

The earliest air-to-surface weapons to be carried by helicopters (such as the previously mentioned Aérospatiale AS 11) were merely adaptations of existing surface-to-surface weapons. This particular missile was steered to its target by means of a joystick transmitting electrical impulses down trailing wires which moved its control surfaces. This obviously required the attacking helicopter to remain in close proximity until its target was hit; a clearly unsatisfactory state of affairs rendering it liable to attack from air or ground.

The AS 11's designated successor, the Aérospatiale AS 12, represented a great step forward; the gunner was only required to track the target with his gunsight, and an infrared sensor would then provide the relevant course corrections. The French dubbed this system TéléCommande Automatique (TCA).

Wire guidance was not completely aban-

doned, however. Hughes' BGM-71 TOW was, as the acronym suggests, Tube-launched, Optically tracked and Wire guided, but also represented a new breed of weapon designed for operation from helicopters. Its gyro-stabilized sight overcame one of the helicopter's biggest problems – vibration. The visual control system was supplanted at night by a Forward-Looking Infra-Red (FLIR) sight with a thermal imaging sensor. The effectiveness of the TOW was illustrated graphically in 1972 when two Bell UH-1s operating in Vietnam accounted for no fewer than 62 targets between them in a single action. TOW was improved by a 5-inch armor-penetrating warhead before it was updated as the 12,000-feet-range TOW 2 and carried by the likes of the AH-1, Westland Lynx, MBB Bö 105, Hughes 500M and others.

The European response to TOW was HOT – a High subsonic Optically-guided Tube-launched missile from Euromissile. With its Venus sighting system mounted in a rotating nose scanner permitting all-weather, all-visibility operation, it was the preferred armament of types like Aérospatiale's Dauphin 2 and Gazelle.

International collaboration was the watchword of the 1970s – at least as far as European manufacturers were concerned. Three military helicopters developed in tandem by

BELOW: A French Army Gazelle unleashes a HOT – High subsonic Optically guided Tube launched – missile, the European weapon manufactured by Aérospatiale of France and MBB of Germany and carried by many different rotary-wing types.

ABOVE: A manufacturers' prototype Aérospatiale Dauphin undergoes sea trials. It is well equipped for naval operation, with advanced, nose-mounted Agrion radar and AS 15 missiles for anti surface vessel attack.

LEFT: The ultimate development of the Aérospatiale Puma medium transport in the mid-1980s was the AS 332B Super Puma, with twin Turbomeca Makila engines. A manufacturer's test airframe is pictured.

Westland and Aérospatiale, as Sud Aviation were now known, proved the decade's most commercially successful types to originate on that side of the Atlantic. The agreement, signed in February 1967, ensured that Europe would be able to compete with the US giants of Bell and Sikorsky, equipping not only the French and British armed forces but achieving significant additional export orders. The development program was said to be the largest ever launched outside the United States – and the results were to prove worthy of such a claim.

The Puma medium transport helicopter and the lighter, all-purpose Gazelle were designated as Aérospatiale types, but were assembled on both sides of the Channel. The Lynx, more powerful than the Gazelle but broadly similar in mission profile, was the only one of the three to boast British design leadership, 70 per cent of the responsibility being carried by Westland. The Puma was similar in appearance to Sud's earlier sub-hunting Super Frelon, but was scaled down in size and power plant (two, instead of three Turboméca Turmo turbines). With a capacity of some 20 troops, its role was primarily transport. The type served both the British and French armed forces (from 1969 and 1971 respectively) in a variety of roles, the Royal Air Force selecting the type to serve alongside, and finally replace the Westland

Wessex. Over 700 machines had been manufactured by the mid-eighties when the type had been developed further.

Engined with two Turboméca Makila turboshafts, each of 1877shp, the resulting AS 332 Super Puma replaced the SA 330B in French service. Saudi Arabia armed the type with Exocet anti-shipping missiles for patrols in the Gulf, while Kuwait ordered a dedicated ASW version with Thomson/CSF Varan radar and Alcatel/Thomson Sintra H212 sonar.

The Super Puma II also became a vehicle for France's highly advanced Orchidée battle-field surveillance radar. This was carried in an underfuselage pod on a rotating mount, being stored when not in use under the junction of fuselage and tail boom. This exceptionally high performance Doppler radar could pinpoint troops and vehicles at ranges of up to 62 miles behind enemy lines while the helicopter was still 31 miles (50km) inside its own lines. Longer main rotor blades with parabolic tips were fitted to a new high-technology rotor head.

The Puma also formed the unofficial basis of an armed helicopter developed by South Africa in the eighties and named Atlas XTP (Experimental Test Program)-1. Stub wings mounted on the cabin sides were the greatest distinguishing feature, with each carrying pods for 18 68mm unguided rockets. South

ABOVE: The Puma (Super Puma pictured) was one of three rotary-wing craft developed and built in partnership by Aérospatiale of France and Westland of Britain. France had design leadership on this and the Gazelle, Westland on the Lynx.

RIGHT: Immediately identifiable by its then-unique 'fenestron' shrouded tail rotor, the Gazelle was intended to fulfil the same observation role for France as the Bell OH-58 Kiowa in the US.

Africa's isolation from the West had obviously not prevented it from developing items like fuel tanks, armored seats, tyres and plastic/composite materials which it could not purchase on the open market. Production versions of the helicopter were reported to feature the standard gunship tandem-seating configuration, with a chin-mounted gun turret, new non-retractable tailwheel landing gear and other refinements. Named Beta, it was expected to enter service alongside South Africa's 50 standard Pumas in the early nineties.

The specification that produced the Gazelle, the French Army's X 300, was originally intended to parallel the successful Light Observation Helicopter that had produced the JetRanger and Hughes OH-6 for the US Army. Much of the type's design bore a resemblance to the Alouette family, though production aircraft showed two distinct differences — the shrouded tail rotor or *fenestron* and the three-bladed semi-articulated rotor. The latter was unusual in that the rotor mast and head formed a single unit, the result being a very respectable performance envelope. The type served warning of its capabilities by establishing three speed records for helicopters in its class in May 1970, while top speed of the production Gazelle nudged 200mph. The type was most usually employed as an observation or forward air control helicopter, directing gunships to their targets, although Gazelles with France and Yugoslavia also acted as tankbusters in the eighties. In the former case, they replaced 70 AS 11-carrying Alouette IIIs as interim gunships, while Yugoslavia armed them with four AT-3 Sagger anti-tank weapons and two SA-7 Grails for air-to-air use should self-defense prove necessary.

BELOW: The speedy Westland Lynx's twin-engine configuration immediately suggested shipboard operation, and was ordered in quantity by the British and French navies.

The Lynx, however, was the most warlike of the three designs, all of which found spin-off uses in the civilian sphere. Its twin-engined specification ideally suited it to shipboard operation, replacing the venerable Wasp that had preceded it from the Westland stable. Performance trials were lengthy, despite a speed record set in 1972 over a 25km course of 199.9mph (321.7kmph) – but once in service with the Royal Navy the type quickly distinguished itself. The shipboard-based Lynx also mounted the British Aerospace Sea Skua, a radar-guided missile optimized for use against patrol boats and other fast-moving surface targets. The French Navy ordered the type to replace the S-58 and Alouette III, both single-engined machines, while in its land-based variant (distinguishable by its skid, rather than four-wheel, undercarriage) it quickly saw service with the British Army Air Corps in Germany.

The Army deployed the Lynx as a tank-buster, flying alongside units of forward air control Gazelles. Armament options were considerable, including a 20mm cannon, Miniguns, up to 36 rockets, or up to six British Aerospace Hawkswing, eight Euromissile HOT or Hughes TOW air-to-surface missiles. As if that wasn't impressive enough, up to eight further missiles could be carried in the cabin for rearming.

Low-level 'nap-of-the-earth' flights practiced by the Lynx in the European theater put amazing stress on both men and machine. With all-weather flight and navigation systems largely automatic, the Lynx combined twin-engined safety with the minimum pilot work-load. In 1986, the type boosted its order book by establishing the world helicopter speed record of 249.09mph. Well over 300 Lynxes were in service in the late eighties, with Brazil, the Netherlands, Nigeria, Egypt and Qatar among the export customers.

The Lynx was set to serve into the next century if the Super Lynx derivative proved

ABOVE: A heavily armed Westland Lynx 3 bristles with air-to-surface missiles. In the last decade, the range of weaponry available for rotorcraft use has often exceeded the sophistication of the airframes themselves, though this is not true of the Lynx.

MIDDLE RIGHT: A Bö-105 armed with the TOW anti-tank guided missile system.

successful. With an extended range and payload and all-weather capability, 360 degree radar, advanced dipping sonar, and powered by 12,120 shp Rolls-Royce Gem engines, it would sport a new high-efficiency tail rotor and a new swept-tip main rotor made from composites. Weapons would include Sea Skua, Penguin and Stingray missiles.

Aérospatiale had also been busy in their own right, following up their successful Alouettes with the smaller Ecureuil and larger Dauphin. It was the latter that found greater application in the military field. The Dauphin 2 was of innovatory construction, with 20 per cent of its structure made up of glassfiber and such substances as Kevlar, Rohacell and Nomex. A further 35 per cent was made from a sandwich of light alloy and Nomex, with a rotor blade of carbon fiber. All

these composite structures added up to strength without weight; it was no surprise when the US Coast Guard broke with tradition to make the Dauphin only the second postwar French design to be bought by the US armed forces. Named Dolphin (a literal translation), the US version contained 60 per cent American components, including twin Avco Lycoming turboshafts.

The Dauphin had been exported to China, who manufactured the type as the Dolphin/Haitun Z-9. Naval versions with magnetic anomaly detection equipment served in the ASW role, while the type also appeared as a military air ambulance. Israel also purchased the Dolphin to fly ASW, fire control and SAR from *Sa'ar* missile boats, while Saudi Arabia specified the Agrion 15 nose radar carried by the French Atlantic maritime patrol aircraft to locate the targets for its four AS 15 air-to-surface missiles carried on outriggers.

An exciting multirole military develop-

TOP: The SA 365F naval version of the Dauphin 2 can perform three maritime roles — attacking surface vessels and submarines, and flying search and rescue operations.

ment of Dauphin 2 was known as SA 365M Panther. It employed exclusively composites for dynamic components and these covered a larger area of the structure — some 15 per cent armored crew seats provided some defense against ground fire, while the airframe was built to withstand a 23 ft/sec crash and the fuel system double that. The Panther also established two impressive world helicopter records when at a weight of 6116

ABOVE: Aerospatiale of France's SA 365K Panther flight tests a pair of 20mm cannon mounted in streamlined pods and intended for fire support missions.

pounds (2774kg) it reached 3000 meters in 2 minutes 54 seconds and 6000 meters in 6 minutes 14 seconds. Operating as an assault transport, it could carry 8-10 troops up to 248 miles. In a gunship role, it sported 22 68mm rockets, 19 2.75mm rockets or a 20mm gun pod. Flying against air targets, it could carry eight Matra Mistral infrared air-to-air missiles or 20mm cannon. The type's impressive development continues.

Bölkow's Bö-103 of 1961 had marked Germany's tentative re-entry to the rotorcraft field it had earlier dominated for so long. Having missed out on a generation of rotorcraft development, however, the manufacturers jumped in at the deep end by specifying a rigid rotor assembly for their first production type. After extensive testing, the Bö-105 (PAH-1) was flown in 1967 as a twin-engined general purpose helicopter. Although it was to achieve success as a tankbuster, it was the type's rotor system that initially attracted world attention. The rigid-

ity of the four-bladed rotor, which was not permitted to flap or drag but change in pitch only, simplified manufacture and battlefield maintenance: but the implications of performance were startling in terms of speed, stability and maneuverability.

Despite a high unit cost, the type proved a success: the West German Heeresflieger (army air arm) ordered 400 machines, 200 for communications and general duties and 200 tankbusters, while the Netherlands, Sudan, the Philippines and Nigeria were among other customers. The type also provided Messerschmitt-Bölkow-Blöhm (as the German manufacturers became) with the rotary-wing experience to develop the BK-117 with the Japanese for the civil market and plan the PAH-2 gunship for the nineties.

The Sikorsky Sea King's development is covered under the heading of anti-submarine warfare, but in truth the design proved far more adaptable than just that. In the civil sphere, the type made millions for Sikorsky

ABOVE: The Sikorsky SH-3, manufactured in Britain as the Westland Sea King, proved enormously successful as a rescue, submarine warfare and executive transport type. Its twin engines and amphibious hull made it ideal for over-water operation.

as the S-61N, the standard passenger-carrying helicopter for commercial routes or oil-rig support, while the design was paid the ultimate compliment when selected as the VH-3A and D to serve with the US Executive Flight Detachment in Washington on Presidential transport duties. Further than this, the S-61 proved to be just the first in a long line of ever more capable military rotorcraft from the Sikorsky stable – most with a decidedly non-maritime mission profile. The seed was sown in 1962 when the US Air Force borrowed a number of SH-3s to service radar units situated off the East Coast of the United States. Initially selected for requisition because of its watertight hull, the SH-3 was so impressive that an Air Force version was rolling off the production line as early as the end of 1963.

Modifications included a hydraulic rear door to facilitate loading of tracked and wheeled vehicles, a retractable tricycle undercarriage to supplement the boat hull, an internal winch and an auxiliary power unit to enable the craft to operate in inhospitable areas with the rotor at rest. Designated S-61R by the manufacturer, the type entered US Air Force service as the CH-3, following the mighty F-4 Phantom as a rare example of a type passing from naval use to the land-based service.

The ruggedness and dependability of the CH-3 was soon put to the test when, as the HH-3E, it was entrusted with the onerous task of penetrating North Vietnamese airspace to rescue shot-down aircrew. Known as 'Jolly Green Giants' after their drab olive camouflage finish, they adopted several refinements: self-sealing fuel tanks and increased armor plating lessened the likelihood of sustaining a fatal hit from random small-arms fire, while a high-speed hoist minimized time in the danger zone. Armament was beefed up courtesy of four Mini-guns, while a retractable in-flight refueling probe enabled range to be maximized.

Refueling *en route* was generally carried out from a sister aircraft, 'buddy'-fashion, though the type boasted sufficient speed in a straight line – 166mph – to utilize a fixed-wing C-130 turboprop tanker. Such was the range this conferred, that two S-61s were able to cross the Atlantic non-stop in 1967, flying to the Paris Air Show courtesy of nine replenishments apiece.

Sikorsky's other sixties' rotorcraft were both smaller and larger than the S-61R. The S-62 (HH-52) replaced the piston-engined H-34/S-58 in US Coast Guard service. In size it was very much a successor to the S-55, whose rotor, control and hydraulic systems it shared, with a General Electric T-58

BELOW: The imposing bulk of a pair of US Marines Sikorsky CH-53s. Developed from the Skycrane, the CH-53 entered Marine Corps service in 1966 and proved an able workhorse in Vietnam where it also served with the US Air Force.

turboshaft offering a dramatic increase in useful load. But despite license production in Japan by Mitsubishi, the type was destined to remain a footnote in Sikorsky's very successful story.

If the S-62's downfall was lack of payload potential, Sikorsky's other project couldn't have been more different. The S-64 (Army designation CH-54) Skycrane was an altogether larger affair – though in terms of fuselage bulk it scarcely amounted to much. Its skeletal frame could accommodate a Universal Military Pod configured as a communications center, surgical unit, command post or a troop-carrying 'people pod'. On other occasions, loads could be underslung – a van carrying 90 troops in combat equipment was one such notable load. In Vietnam the CH-54 was tasked with recovery of downed rotorcraft of all kinds, most frequently the ubiquitous UH-1. It had its Soviet counterpart in the Mil Mi-10 Harke, a larger but substantially similar machine. This appeared to the West in 1961, one year before Sikorsky's Skycrane flew and, like the S-64, was to see limited commercial application in oil pipeline laying, etc. Its biggest advantage over the US type was the ability to double as a troop carrier, 28 passengers being accommodated in an abbreviated fuselage.

Mil's line of heavy lift military helicopters had flourished since the successful Mi-4. By far the largest was the Mi-6, flown in September 1957 and for a long time the world's largest production helicopter. To emphasize its size, its gearbox and rotor head weighed twice that of its predecessor, the Mi-4. In exceeding a speed in level flight of 300km/h (186mph) on the power of two 5500 shp Sovloviev turbine engines, the Mi-6 was awarded

In a slightly less radical vein, the Mi-8 medium transport paralleled the example of the S-58 by marrying turboshaft power to a proven rotor and mechanical assembly – the Mi-4, naturally. Code-named Hip by NATO, the result entered service in 1967 and saw service with a score of countries both within and without the Warsaw Pact. A 28-seater in transport configuration, it proved its versatility when Egypt used the type in 1974 as a minesweeper in attempting to clear the Suez Canal, while it was also observed serving as an interim gunship with the wire-guided AT-3 Sagger missile. Yet a fuel system that could be rendered inoperative by a single leak suggested that the Mi-8 would prove as much a liability on the battlefield as an asset.

The Mi-8 was also developed into a very effective anti-submarine helicopter, the Mi-14 Haze. Another less publicised update to the Mi-8 was the Mi-17 Hip-H, revealed in 1981 as a Mi-8 re-engined with the uprated power plant used by the Mi-14 and Mi-24 (two Isotov TV3-117 turboshafts rated at 1900 shp apiece). Armed with 23mm GSH gun packs as found on variants of Hind, together with defensive armor plate, they have been used as gunships in Afghanistan and South America.

ABOVE: The three-engined CH-53E Super Stallion was fast enough to utilize the services of a C-130 fixed-wing tanker.

LEFT: Sikorsky's S-62 was one of its less successful helicopters. Designated HH-52A by the US military, it replaced the S-58/H-34 in US Coast Guard service and was also built in Japan.

the Igor Sikorsky International Trophy in 1961, assisted by two variable-incidence winglets attached to the fuselage offloading the rotor. Three years later it set a speed record for a 100km closed circuit of 340kmph (211mph), an achievement that remained unmatched in 1989.

Although ostensibly developed to help exploit the Soviet Union's barren wastes, the military possibilities of its 26,000 pound payload were soon evident. At the 1961 Tushino Air Display, six Mi-6s landed in two groups: one of each group carried a pair of artillery missiles, complete with transporters, the others the associated personnel and equipment. Alternative loads included tanks or armored personnel carriers, the latter being deployed most successfully in Ethiopia in 1978. Configured as a troop transport with rear-facing seats, 65 passengers could be accommodated. Whatever its internal or external load, the Mi-6 was indeed a formidable transport helicopter for the West to consider.

ABOVE: Pictured in an interim gunship role, the Mil Mi-8 was more often seen as a 28- seat medium transport which entered service in 1967 and has since been widely exported.

The H-3's success in Vietnam suggested a need for an even larger, more powerful helicopter to fulfill the rescue role. And once more Sikorsky's designers were equal to the task. Though it outwardly resembled the S-61/H-3 series, their S-65/H-53 series owed more in terms of mechanical components to the previously mentioned Skycrane. Exceeding the H-3 in rotor diameter and fuselage length by 10 feet in either direction, and with similar armor and equipment, plus uprated General Electric T64 turboshafts, it rapidly took up where its predecessor had left off on

ABOVE: Mil's mighty Mi-6 underlines its 26,000-pound load-carrying capacity by lifting a prefabricated building. In wartime, the underslung load could just as easily be a tank, a field gun or an armored personnel carrier.

its entrance to US Marine Corps service in late 1966. The following year saw USAF CH-53B variants serving alongside the CH-3E in Vietnam, where the Aerospace Rescue and Recovery service had carved out an important niche in the US order of battle. In a pure transport role, rear loading doors, winches and roller track combined to accommodate the likes of a 1.5 ton truck and trailer, a 105mm howitzer or an Honest John missile.

The type then reverted to its naval origins, being adopted by the US Navy as the service's standard minesweeping helicopter. Designated RH-53D in production form, this variant was able to deal with magnetic, acoustic and mechanical mines with equal facility. The former two varieties of mine were detonated by towing a 'sled' across the surface of the water to simulate the passage of a vessel. Explosive charges could also be used in a controlled attempt to cut loose mines moored to the sea bed.

The ultimate and most impressive vari-

ation on Sikorsky's theme came in the imposing shape of the CH-53E. Adding 50 per cent more power to the standard CH-53 via the expedient of a third engine, the type doubled its predecessor's lifting potential. A seven-blade rotor made from titanium and glassfiber combined with this to produce so much torque that the tail fin and rotor was canted 20 degrees from the vertical to help counterbalance the forces acting upon it. Such power enabled enormous load potential to be realized; indeed, the CH-53E was impressive in its own right. It was by far the heaviest helicopter yet flown outside the USSR on the second prototype's maiden flight in 1974.

The US Navy's minesweeper development, the MH-53E, featured enlarged stabilizing sponsons, each with a 500 US gallon fuel capacity, these endowing the type with a 20-hour-plus endurance. Meanwhile, the US Marine Corps seemed happy to rewrite the military strategy book: the CH-53E could

RIGHT: The Mi-6 here displays the Clamshell rear-loading doors to its capacious hold. The detachable fixed wing also visible on these examples was intended to offload the rotor in forward flight when the helicopter was heavily laden.

ABOVE: The Sikorsky H-53 series was adopted by the US Navy for minesweeping duties, serving in ever more capable RH-53D, MH-53WE and MH-53E variants.

transport 98 per cent of USMC aircraft undismantled while, when configured as a troop carrier, it could accommodate 55 persons or airlift 93 per cent of a US Marine Division's combat items.

Sikorsky's ultimate Sea King developments took the aircraft into an amazing fourth decade of development and service — and arguably deserved the 'supercopter' tag. The MH-53E Sea Dragon mine counter-

measures version of the Super Stallion could tow mechanical, acoustic and magnetic hydrofoil gear through the water. Meanwhile, Sikorsky was modifying CH-53 Super Jolly Green Giants to MH-53J status with Pave Low Enhanced Technology, upgrading the combat rescue and recovery fleet for USAF Special Operations Forces. The Sea King and its relations had come a very long way indeed.

Just as early German helicopters had acted as an airborne 'crow's nest' to see over the horizon, it was inevitable that the helicopter would one day seek foes under the surface as well as on it. The advantages were obvious. While fixed-wing aircraft could rarely stay on station to make accurate readings a possibility, and surface vessels were themselves likely targets for their foe, the helicopter could take readings from a hovering position, its safety assured unless the submarine should risk all by breaking surface.

The anti-submarine helicopter seldom worked totally alone. All anti-submarine operations by rotary-wing craft would typically come under the control of a fixed-wing airborne command post such as the Nimrod (in RAF service) or the US Navy's Lockheed P-3 Orion. Surveying the scene from altitude, this would be in the best position to make tactical decisions, deploying sub-hunting helicopters like so many chessmen. The majority of anti-submarine helicopters were purpose-built machines, primarily due to the fact that modifying existing types to suit the requirements of shipboard operation would quite often be as costly as conceiving an entirely new design. These requirements included folding tail and rotor assembly for shipboard storage in the minimum possible space; castoring undercarriage members to permit landing from any direction; navigation and stabilization systems that could operate in all weather and visibility conditions; and a strong, weather- and water-resistant structure. The turbine permitted extended operation at something like 85 per cent of maximum power. This allowed extended hovering on station, for example, when dunking sonar – an important consideration. The turbine's high cost was a relatively unimportant factor.

Two means of detection had been pioneered in the hunt for the ever-elusive submarine. The helicopter was ideally placed to take advantage of both. First to be developed was MAD or Magnetic Anomaly Detection. This operated on the principle that a submarine's presence in the water could be detected by means of its deviation from the earth's standard magnetic field. This device was found to be effective in detecting submarines at a depth of up to 300 feet, but there was one considerable disadvantage – it had a very short range, obliging the hunting aircraft to maintain a height above sea level of 100 feet or less. Fixed-wing aircraft were thus faced with the problem of how to press home an attack while flying away at speed – a dilemma eliminated by hovering. Another practical problem with this method of detection was that since the aircraft itself was

metal, accurate magnetic anomaly readings could only be obtained by distancing the 'bird' from the airframe (usually by towing it). The helicopter's ability to hover and move at a comparatively slow speed enabled better use to be made of magnetic anomaly detection. More promising, however, was sonar.

Originally developed between the wars as Asdic, Sonar operated on an acoustic basis. Hydrophones had been used in a limited way for some while, typically being fitted to the hull of a flying boat to listen, microphone-like, for sounds transmitted through the water. Now the American-developed sonobuoy combined a hydrophone with a transmitter, enabling any sounds produced to be relayed for as long as the batteries survived. Ranges of up to three and a half miles were attainable under good conditions, although

CHAPTER FOUR

The Sub-Hunters

directional or distance information was unavailable from passive sonar. The disadvantage of dropping sonobuoys in the sea was obvious: moving with the prevailing current, their position would not be fixed and any reading obtained could not therefore be accurately assessed. Furthermore, although many were fitted with a soluble bung to submerge the sonobuoy and prevent it falling into enemy hands, the operation was at best wasteful.

Active sonar, by contrast, sent out impulses and measured the reflection (if any) from a submerged enemy, rather in the same way as dolphins locate their food. By suspending a sonobuoy below the helicopter, readings could be taken from a number of carefully calculated locations, resulting in a cross-referencing pattern. This transformed the nature of anti-submarine warfare at a stroke: the helicopter had finally given surface forces the whip hand.

The US Navy employed unmanned drones

OPPOSITE: A US Navy Sikorsky SH-3H of Squadron HS-4 dips its sonar. The information obtained by submerging a sonobuoy on a retractable cable was to prove of inestimable value in locating the hidden submarine menace – and the SH-3 was one of the premier hunter/killer types.

in their DASH (Drone Anti-Submarine Helicopter) weapons system in an attempt to prolong the life of World War II-vintage destroyers. The chosen vehicle was Gyrodyne's QH-50, a crude-looking contraption of tubular steel with a 300 shp Boeing T50 shaft turbine. After successful deck landing trials in 1960, the radio-controlled QH-50 entered service in 1962: by 1966, over 300 had been built and were serving on some 90 ships. An interesting sidelight on the co-axial rotor QH-50 was its method of directional control via air-drag rotor-tip brakes. Two homing torpedoes could be underslung and delivered within the type's operational range of 70 miles. Unsophisticated the QH-50 certainly was, but it performed a useful stop-gap function at minimal cost.

Two strains of sub-hunting helicopter from either side of the Iron Curtain initially shared certain similarities. Charles H Kaman and Nikolai Kamov had both persevered with twin rotors — in Kaman's case intermeshing, his 'rival' Kamov preferring co-axial blades. Both these unusual layouts had the benefit of producing helicopters which, requiring no compensatory tail rotor to counteract torque, could dispense with long-drawn-out tail assemblies: the advantages for shipboard storage were evident.

Kaman's designs sprung from the HTK-1 trainer and HOK-1 observation helicopter ordered by the Navy and Marine Corps respectively. But he forsook the format completely to create the SH-2 Seasprite, which started life as a utility helicopter with an amphibious capability. Its capacious cabin could accommodate 11 passengers, and when the addition of a second General Electric T-58 turboshaft improved performance radically

ABOVE: Massive fuel-filled sponson floats identify this three-engined monster as a MH-53E Sea Dragon, last in a line of H-3 developments from Sikorsky.

LEFT: A large ventral radome identifies this Sea King sub-hunter as modified to fulfil an Airborne Early Warning role.

RIGHT: Kamov KA-25 Hormone ASW helicopters pictured on board the Soviet anti-submarine cruiser *Moskva*.

BELOW: A Kaman SH-2F Seasprite LAMPS helicopter, comes in to land. Re-engined and updated from its original UH-2A form of 1962, the Seasprite proved capable of over 20 years' service.

the type was perceived as an interim LAMPS (Light Airborne Multi-Purpose System) contender.

The Navy's specification combined two major roles, both of vital importance in the defense of surface vessels: anti-submarine warfare (ASW) and anti-ship surveillance and targeting (ASST). The lightweight prefix indicated an ability to operate from the US Navy's smaller ships of the frigate, destroyer

and cruiser categories. Ship-to-helicopter communications were to be of paramount importance. Upgrading to SH-2F standard involved considerable modification — search radar, homing torpedoes, a MAD bird — but the result was a helicopter that served well into the eighties to notch up over two decades of useful life.

Kamov, meanwhile, stayed true to his chosen configuration to find even greater success in serving the Soviet Navy. His first designs were reminiscent of the Focke Achgelis unpowered autogiros, being towed behind surface vessels for observation. The experimental, powered Ka-8 and Ka-10 were followed by the larger and more capable Ka-15 in 1952. A side-by-side two-seater, the latter's diminutive fuselage length of 19 feet 6 inches made it a natural choice for shipboard duties. It was followed into limited service with the Soviet naval air arm (AVMF) by the Ka-18 (1958), which fulfilled a general purpose role. In replacing the Mi-1, it was said to possess double the range of its predecessor for nearly half the fuselage length.

But it was the Ka-25 with which Kamov made his greatest mark. Code-named Hormone, it made its public debut in 1961, and thereafter served as the Soviet navy's main anti-submarine helicopter, replacing the non-optimized Mi-4 in this role. While not

LEFT: The Ka-25 was deployed in sub-hunting (Hormone-A) and radar picket/ missile guidance (Hormone-B) variants aboard Soviet vessels; the latter is pictured here.

quite matching the Ka-18's size-to-range claim, the Ka-25 proved successful enough to kill off any challenge from Mil, whose design bureau thenceforth concentrated on land-based types.

Hormone's twin 900 shp Glushenkov turboshafts, each with its own fuel supply, provided a crucial safety margin for a type four times as heavy as the preceding Ka-18. The foreshortened fuselage belied the fact that in weight – if not length – the type most nearly resembled the Sikorsky S-58. Two versions were deployed aboard the Soviet fleet, the Hormone-A anti-submarine helicopter and the Hormone-B radar picket/missile guidance variant.

The Ka-25 was operated in large numbers, its total deployment of 150 during the eighties making it the most widely used Soviet naval aircraft of all. Aside from its own pair of acoustic homing torpedo armament, the Ka-25A could transmit data to enable use of the surface-to-surface SS-N-14 anti-submarine missile carried by *Moskva* and *Kiev* class ships. In its Hormone-B variant, it enabled older surface-to-surface missiles like the SS-N-3 and the more modern SS-N-12 to be guided beyond the range of the parent ship's radar – and with a ceiling of 16,500 feet, the Ka-25 could extend the range of these anti-ship missiles quite considerably.

With Kamov cornering the market in Soviet shipborne rotorcraft, Mil's belated development of the Mi-8 as an ASW helicopter came as some surprise. Most examples of the Mi-14 were operated from land. First flown in 1973, the type entered Soviet service some four years later. Haze-A was the designation of the ASW version with a retractable sonar

and weapons bay at the bottom of the boat hull. This gave it a remarkable visual similarity to the S-61/H-3 family: one could only wonder why it had taken so long to appear, given that nearly 20 years had elapsed since the appearance of the parent type in 1961. Nevertheless, the Mi-14 proved a useful successor to the Mi-4, although Kamov retained shipboard superiority due to the Ka-25's relatively small size.

Haze-B was a mine countermeasures helicopter with a starboard fuselage pod and lacking Haze-A's distinctive MAD 'bird' stowed under the tail. The Soviet, East German and Polish navies all operated this variant in small numbers. Haze-C added a double-width sliding door to the port side of the cabin to provide a search and rescue equivalent of the Sea King for Russia and Poland. A further distinguishing feature was the searchlight on either side of the nose.

The helicopter's limited range and payload capabilities had always necessitated operation in hunter/killer pairs, one detecting the sub, the other deploying its weapons against it. The advent of the turbine engine, of course, changed all this. Westland's re-engining of the Sikorsky S-58 enabled hunting and killing functions to be combined.

Sikorsky, meanwhile, designed the Sea King specifically to combine both roles in the same airframe. First flown in March 1959, it entered US Navy service two-and-a-half years later with submarine hunter units VHS-3 based at Norfolk, Virginia, and VHS-10 at Ream Field, San Diego. One Sea King, it was reckoned, could do the job of two piston-engined S-58s, hunting down the submarine and killing it. In terms of submarine

RIGHT: Sikorsky's Sea King in its SH-3H variant on board USS *Nimitz*. With homing torpedo and depth charges on board as well as sonar and search radar, this was a true sub hunter/killer in one airframe.

RIGHT: After their successes with the Whirlwind and Wessex, Westland undertook license production of the SH-3 Sea King from the late 1960s. This is an HAS Mark 5 aircraft from No. 706 Squadron, Royal Navy.

detection, the Sea King had much to offer, carrying both sonar and Doppler search radar. A radar altimeter facilitated precision hovering for accurate dipping sonar readings, while an offensive load of some 840 pounds could include homing torpedoes and depth charges.

Twin 1250 (later 1400) shp General Electric T58 shaft turbines afforded not only a good performance envelope but increased safety margins that would permit flying without a partner. And should a double engine failure occur, the fully watertight boat-section hull – another considerable advantage over the S-58 it was scheduled to replace – would permit indefinite survival. The type was even able to be operated from water, though in practice this was a relatively little-used capability. The S-61/H-3 Sea King proved the basis for a whole family of very capable transport helicopters, their missions quite different from the ASW role the type was originally designed to fulfill. These developments are described elsewhere.

Soviet strategy in anti-submarine warfare was based around deployment of the *Kiev*-class VTOL carrier, which with its complement of Kamov Ka-25 and Ka-27 helicopters and Yakovlev Yak-36 Forgers represented, in the late Admiral Sergei Gorshkov's opinion, 'The most powerful force intended

for search and destruction of enemy nuclear-powered submarines in distant ocean areas.' While the West could predict areas through which Soviet nuclear submarines would have to pass, such as the Greenland-Iceland-UK gap in the North Atlantic, the Soviet Union had no such advantage, and had therefore to be able to provide a flexible response to any threat. Furthermore, the average Western submarine made much less noise than its Soviet counterpart, making detection that much more difficult. In spite of security leaks from the West which have enabled the Soviet Union to update her sonar equipment, it would be fair to assume that the level of sophistication of Soviet sub-hunting devices remained inferior to that of, say, the United States. The likes of *Kiev* could attempt to shadow US nuclear submarines from their bases on the East Coast, operating under the watchful eye of the Tu-20 Bear-F long-range command aircraft. But the Soviet task was still significantly more difficult than that facing their adversary.

The development of all-capable types like the Sea King still left a gap at the lower end of the market for helicopters that could operate more modestly from platforms at the stern of frigates, etc. By the 1970s, most escort vessels had the capability to operate helicopters, with most adding a weatherproof hangar/

RIGHT: Agusta's single-seat A 106 existed simply to carry the two Mark 44 torpedoes visible under its body – yet the anti-submarine capability it added to *Impavido*-class vessels of the Italian Navy was invaluable.

BELOW: The Kamov Ka-27 Helix, long-awaited Hormone successor which was first noted by the West in 1981. More capable than its predecessor, Helix nevertheless retained the Hormone's dimensions to facilitate shipboard operation.

the twin-engined Bell UH-1N as the AB-212 introduced a new and extremely capable ASW helicopter to the scene. Although optimized for anti-submarine work, the type displayed all the multi-purpose hallmarks of the UH-1 'Huey' family. With simple alterations to internal layout, the type could serve as a troop transport and fire support helicopter or air ambulance, for liaison or in an Electronic Countermeasures role, with a crew of up to four (two pilots, two radar/electronic officers). The AB-212ASW offered them a special cockpit display featuring all the flight information needed for each phase of the ASW operation.

The largest helicopter built by France at the time of its debut, Sud Aviation's Super Frelon, emerged as an anti-submarine force having been conceived originally as an assault transport helicopter. Its sheer size — 56 feet with blades and tail folded — limited its deployment to aircraft carriers, but with a

ABOVE: The Bell 212, one of the more sophisticated developments of the original Model 204/ UH-1 Huey. Agusta of Italy supplied the European market, while their AB 212ASW was a particularly capable anti-submarine package.

workshop to the rudimentary helipad.

Agusta were quick to fill this gap with their miniature A 106, a single-seat high performance helicopter designed purely and simply as a delivery system for two Mark 44 torpedoes slung underneath its body. With a length (rotor and tail folded) of just 22 feet 8 inches, it found a home on the *Impavido*-class ships of the Italian Navy, supplementing the Marinavia's larger types. Curiously enough, Agusta had a monopoly on the production of these with license-built versions of Sikorsky and Bell products. Yet their development of

crew of four, sonar and search radar in the stabilizing floats it had all the qualifications — not to mention an enviable four-hour endurance. Israel used the type on land as an assault transport, a role in which it also proved very effective.

As so often, the US Navy was at the forefront of development, conceiving a design competition to equip them with a LAMPS helicopter for the eighties. A Sikorsky design was selected to fulfill this task but, as already mentioned, the interim LAMPS role was filled by the Kaman Seasprite, adding

ABOVE: An SH-60B Seahawk with MAD anomaly detection lands on board a US frigate.

RIGHT: Sud Aviation's SA 321 Super Frelon, one of the world's largest anti-submarine helicopters, also doubled as a 30-troop assault transport with France, South Africa and Israel.

ABOVE: A Kaman Seasprite, a widely-used anti submarine helicopter.

many extra years of service to an already illustrious career.

The eventual winner, dubbed the Seahawk, was an adapted version of the Sikorsky S-70, already in US Army service as the H-60A Black Hawk. Selected after a fly-off against the Boeing Vertol H-61 in 1974, its naval modifications as compared with its land-based forebear make for interesting reading. Firstly, the distance between main and tail-wheel was reduced by a surprising 46 per cent, moving the latter from the furthest extent of the fuselage to a point inboard. This shorter 'wheelbase' was essential to make deck landing easier. For ease of shipboard storage, the tailplane and main rotor blades were hinged. Armor plating – and thus weight – was reduced, an in-flight refueling probe added to increase time on station, and full maritime avionics installed.

In the early 1990s, Sikorsky's Seahawk was being further developed by Mitsubishi Japan. Japanese avionics and equipment including ring giro AHRS, data link, tactical data processing and automatic flight management systems were being integrated by the Japan defense agency. The first helicopters of this type based on imported airframes were flown in 1987: up to 100 were under order, excluding 40 simpler search and rescue machines.

Despite its involvement in the Hokum heli-

copter fighter project that was keeping NATO on its toes in the late eighties, the Kamov bureau maintained its keen interest in shipboard ASW helicopters in the shape of the Ka-27 Helix. First seen in 1981 in the Baltic Sea on board *Udaloy*, the first Soviet guided missile destroyer, Helix was very similar in overall dimensions to its predecessor and could therefore fly from all classes of ship that had previously operated the Ka-25.

Some 60 examples of Helix-A, the standard ASW variant, had entered service by the late eighties, while eight had been supplied to India as the Ka-28. The Ka-27 Helix-B provided missile guidance over the horizon for the parent ship's surface-to-surface missiles. A sea-based amphibious assault variant also existed, as did Helix-D, a search and rescue/plane guard derivative seen on board *Novorossiysk*.

With the nuclear submarine a major player in the strategic game on which our peace and security depends, the continuing development of the sub-hunting helicopter was as assured as anything in warfare. Developments in the nineties are more likely to emerge in the weaponry and avionics fields than in any startlingly new airframes: indeed, the specter of standardization suggests that ASW helicopters of the future are likely to resemble already successful land-based types.

As military equipment grew in complexity in the postwar era, so the costs escalated in (or sometimes out of) proportion. The rotary-wing sector was no different, and the seventies and eighties saw increasing international co-operation in a bid to keep one step ahead of current trends. The rotorcraft had, in less than a quarter of a decade, graduated from a peripheral player to a vital means of ensuring battlefield supremacy. Yet as gunships, tactical transports and submarine hunter/killers brought their specialist skills to bear, so this specialization increased costs. While the sixties had seen helicopters developed to fulfill specific roles, so the eighties would see the return of the all-purpose rotorcraft.

The Superpowers, the Soviet Union and United States, continued to plow their own development furrows . . . though in the late-eighties period of *perestroika*, it seemed likely that a decreasing proportion of the Soviet budget would be made available for military spending purposes. The importance of retaining a stake in rotary-wing development was nowhere illustrated more clearly than at Britain's Westland Helicopters, where a takeover battle between America's Sikorsky and a European consortium cost two Government ministers their posts.

With Vietnam now history, the focus of attention invariably centered on the European theater and Germany in particular as the likely battleground for a future major war. Meanwhile, outbreaks in the Falklands and Afghanistan provided pointers to future problems and future solutions.

The Falklands saw specialized sea-to-land operations, proving the sense of not dispensing with carriers entirely. Types as diverse as the Scout, Wessex and Chinook were employed in the respective roles of communications, troop transport and heavy lift, while Royal Navy Lynxes acted as air guards.

In a future European conflict, it was assumed that helicopters would not only be deployed against static or mobile ground targets but also against each other. It was therefore important to be able to avoid detection, press home attacks independently and, if hit by a ground-to-air missile, have the ability to survive as much battle damage as possible.

The helicopter's main means of concealment was still nap-of-the-earth flying, maintaining a constant low altitude in an attempt to avoid radar detection. This was obviously wearing on both man and machine, with constant course and height corrections necessary. Head-up displays were one answer, projecting details of speed, altitude and heading into the pilot's field of vision. In terms of weapons technology, the trend was towards 'fire and forget' missiles which, once locked on to a target, needed no further control from the helicopter.

And while the danger of attack from the ground was ever-present, survivability was a priority when such advanced technology was at stake. The ultimate in disposable helicopters had to be the remotely piloted drone, and it was not surprising when this made a comeback as a relatively cheap and ultimately expendable battlefield surveillance vehicle. Canadair were just one company pursuing this route as the eighties closed.

It was also possible that fixed-wing types such as the tankbusting Fairchild A-10 could be vulnerable to attack from helicopters operating above the battlefield: significantly in this respect there have been reports of the SA-7 Grail (usually operated surface-to-air)

CHAPTER FIVE

Supercopters

being added to the Hind's armament. But such a missile would only be of use against a low, slow-flying opponent: a new generation of missiles was on the way to take the 'hit and hope' element out of helicopter warfare.

In the search for a battlefield attack helicopter to serve in the European theater, the weapon actually came before the aircraft. The Rockwell AGM-114 Hellfire (the name an acronym of HELicopter Launched FIRE and forget) was intended to take helicopter-borne anti-tank weaponry to a new plateau. Unlike the previous generation of wire-guided missiles, Hellfire could, as its name intimated, be fired without the need to wait for the kill — and with helicopter gunships of both sides simultaneously active over the battlefield, the advantage was obvious. Laser designation was the means by which the missile would find the target, flying down a ribbon of reflected light shone from either the launching helicopter or another less vulnerable aircraft.

OPPOSITE: The AH-64 Apache took the helicopter gunship concept to new heights of sophistication, with outstanding weapons systems and exceptional survivability for the crew through advanced construction techniques.

ABOVE: A British Army Air Corps Lynx armed with Hellfire missiles. Laser designation negated the need for wire guidance, making the weapon a true advance in battlefield combat.

Although the missile underwent tests with the likes of the Black Hawk and HueyCobra, there was to be an entirely new helicopter built as its platform. Known as the Advanced Attack Helicopter (AAH) and the subject of an intensive mid-seventies design competition, this was the Hughes (later McDonnell Douglas) AH-64 Apache. Selected in preference to the Bell AH-63, the sinister-looking Apache represented a significant development from the HueyCobra in size and sophistication: all-weather operation was a crucial component of the mission profile. The tandem seating arrangement with pilot amidships pioneered by the AH-1 was retained — but in almost every other respect the AH-64 wrote its own specification.

With such advanced technology on board, it was essential that the AH-64 had every possible chance to make it back to base even if heavy battle damage had been sustained. With this in mind, the main rotor and fuel tank were subjected to repeated hits from 23mm ammunition simulating Soviet artillery: this they survived. Crucially, too, the Black Hole infrared suppressor system developed by Hughes themselves made the task of infrared heat-seeking missiles significantly more difficult by cooling and diffusing engine exhaust — a problem the Mil Mi-24 had in Afghanistan. If all else failed and the Apache was downed, an estimated 95 per cent of crashes at an amazing 42 feet per second were reckoned to be survivable by its two-man crew.

Weapon control was courtesy of the Target Acquisition and Designation Sight (TADS) mounted in the aircraft's nose. The sophistication of the system was impressive: TADS combined a TV camera and laser rangefinder as its sighting mechanisms, with infrared backup for night work and for operations in poor visibility. Also mounted in the nose, the Pilot's Night Vision Sensor (PNVS) presented the helicopter's airspeed, altitudes and heading on a monocle-style eyeglass, beaming information from its location amidships in the avionics bay.

By the late 1980s, the Apache bore the McDonnell Douglas name; in 1987 the company announced development of an Advanced Apache, with advanced avionics and fly-by-wire controls, a Honeywell ring-laser inertial navigation system, 2000 shp T700 engines, rearward-looking TV and air-to-air Stinger missiles. The latter, it was

LEFT: A Westland Scout unleashes an air-to-surface missile. Advanced weapons technology was often applied to obsolescent airframes in an attempt to create interim gunships pending the arrival of more sophisticated rotorcraft.

RIGHT: A development example of the Apache is put through its paces. Hellfire missiles and rocket pods are visible on its stub wing, with a Target Acquisition and Designation Sight in the nose controlling the weapons.

BELOW: The Advanced Apache, announced in 1987, was more capable still with Stinger missiles.

claimed, would be 'slaved' to the gunner's helmet for off-axis firing – an interesting and potentially groundbreaking advance in helicopter armament. Despite all this innovation, there would be 75 per cent commonality with the basic Apache – a crucial point manufacturers had never forgotten since the ill-fated Lockheed Cheyenne fell to the Huey-Cobra. The Advanced Apache was also being proposed to fill the German PAH-2 attack helicopter requirement.

The Soviet response to the AH-64 came in the shape of the Mil Mi-28 Havoc. Although details of this type remained a closely guarded secret for most of the 1980s, there were clear indications that it would prove to be a significant type. When the Mil Mi-28 was finally unveiled to the West in summer 1989, it appeared that 'the heavy beast' – as its own designers had mockingly yet accurately dubbed it – had body armor that made it fully three tons heavier than its Western rival. It lacked the advanced guidance and radar systems of the AH-64, but many observers judged on first acquaintance that the package could be more effective.

It was a threat the West certainly took seriously – and when the US Army's Sergeant York mobile anti-aircraft gun was abandoned in 1985 it was largely due to the Mi-28. The gun's 4km effective range was not enough as Caspar Weinberger, then Defense Secretary, stated: 'A helicopter that can stand off at six kilometers and fire lethal fire into troops maneuvering or taking part in combat requires a defense system that can do the same.' Havoc was believed to feature sophisticated systems similar to the AH-64, these being housed under the nose in an electro-optical pod enclosing LLTV (Low Light TV)

ABOVE: The sharp end of Mil's Mi-28 Havoc as revealed at the Paris Salon in June 1989. Heavier and probably more capable than the AH-64, Havoc was well respected by NATO.

LEFT: A West German MBB Bö-105 armed with HOT missiles amidships. Messerschmitt were collaborating with Aérospatiale in the early 1990s to produce the Bö-105's intended replacement, the PAH-2.

and/or a laser designator and marked target seeker. A heavy caliber gun under the fuselage, up to 16 anti-tank missiles, rockets and other external stores could be carried.

The likelihood of a European anti-tank helicopter challenging the AH-64's design supremacy rested largely in the hands of Messerschmitt and Aérospatiale, who joined forces to produce contenders for each country's armed force's specifications. The German PAH-2 and French HAC-1 seemed certain to be filled by the fruits of this liaison, named Eurocopter.

Beating this collaboration to the punch was the Agusta A 129 Mangusta, a totally new attack helicopter from the Italian company that had achieved most success with license-built designs. The Mangusta (Mongoose) made use of certain components and systems from the already successful A 109 civil helicopter – a commonality that assisted in its three-year dash from first flight in 1983 to entering service with the Italian Army. Powered by two Rolls-Royce Gem turbines, the A 129 could boast an extremely light and strong main rotor, combining a glassfiber spar with a composite skin to provide a significant survival rate when peppered with 12.7mm ammunition. As a latecomer on the gunship scene, the A 129 was prepared for all eventualities, with stub-wing attachment points for eight Hughes TOW, eight HOT or six Hellfire anti-tank missiles. And although avionics and systems were not as sophisticated as the Hughes AH-64, performance was well up to expectation. Italy's ability to produce a small, potent attack helicopter such as this was undeniably impressive.

The Mangusta gave birth to a potentially important second-generation development:

the joint European helicopter (JEH) project backed by Agusta, CASA, Fokker and Westland. Shareholdings were 38 per cent each to Agusta and Westland (already collaborators on the EH 101 project), 19 per cent to Fokker and 5 per cent to CASA. Named after an ancient Aztec god, the A 129 LAH Tonal was clearly based on the helicopter whose designation it had borrowed, but would have weapons systems to enable it to fill the anti-tank, scout and anti-helicopter roles. Third generation anti-tank and anti-aircraft weapons would be employed, with the option of gun and rocket backup. Intended to enter service in 1997, the Tonal is intended to serve in the following numbers: UK 125, Italy 90, Netherlands 50 and Spain 40. Though no new airframe existed in 1989, a modified A 129 was being used to demonstrate the new helicopter's configuration.

ABOVE: Agusta's A 109 in military garb. The Argentine Army flew the type as an anti-tank gunship in the Falklands conflict, with other air arms using it as a transport, ASW or Scout type.

LEFT: The first prototype of the Agusta A 129 Mangusta attack helicopter pictured in 1984 and (above) the state of the art gunner's cockpit.

TOP: A civil example of Agusta's A 109, a type so versatile that it was modified to perform many varied military roles after first finding favor as a police helicopter.

ABOVE: A Westland EH 101 in flight. Developed in collaboration with Italy's Agusta, the three-engined type was intended to replace Puma in the Royal Air Force, as well as picking up orders from Italy and Canada.

with Mathogo anti-tank missiles, and at least one of these helicopters was captured by the RAF during the Falklands conflict.

Since the early eighties, light attack, aerial scout and target designation variants had been flown. As a naval anti-surface vessel and anti-submarine type, it was equipped with MAD, a pair of homing torpedoes and a high-performance radar capable of high discrimination in rough sea conditions. Most interesting variant of the A 109, however, was the so-called 'Mirach' machine carrying two remotely piloted vehicles of the same name for battlefield surveillance, reconnaissance, target acquisition, electronic intelligence, electronic countermeasures and the saturation of enemy defense.

Continuing the theme of European co-operation, Westland and Agusta joined forces as EHI to develop the EH 101 – a helicopter that was slightly smaller in size than Sea King but could boast a substantially increased load thanks to three General Electric T700 turboshafts. Developed from the Westland WG 34 design project of the late 1970s, it was due to roll off the two production lines in Italy and the UK in 1991, with deliveries to both navies projected that same year. It beat the Super Puma to Canada's Sea King replacement, the NSA (New Shipborne Aircraft), and would also serve the Royal Air Force as a 35-troop tactical transport, augmenting and then replacing the Puma in this role.

The Eurocopter company was formed when Germany's Messerschmitt-Bölkow-Blöhm and France's Aérospatiale decided to meet their countries' different specifications for an anti-tank helicopter for the next century with variants of the same machine. The German specification, labeled PAH-2 (Panzerabwehr-hubschrauber, 2nd generation) was intended to provide an anti-tank capability for the German army from 1998 onwards. The type's semi-rigid rotor was driven by two MTU/Rolls-Royce/Turboméca MTM 390s mounted side by side, each yielding 1284 shp. Armament consisted of eight HOT anti-tank missiles, plus four Stingers for self-defense in the air.

France's HAC (Hélicoptère Anti-Char) version was also intended to enter service in 1998. Its impressive mast-mounted TV/Forward Looking Infra Red/tracker/laser rangefinder served the gunner, while a pilot-operated FLIR helmet sight backed it up in case of the gunner being knocked out in combat. In tandem with the HAC, Eurocopter were developing a Hélicoptère d'Appui Protection, an escort and fire support version for the French Army to enter service in 1997. Formidably armed with 30mm GIAT cannon, four Matra Mistral air-to-air missiles and 22 SNEB rockets, it also featured roof-mounted

It was noticeable that development times of many new helicopters were scheduled for as much as a decade from drawing board to deployment. Such was the delay in the case of the Tonal that the Dutch army were in 1989 negotiating for 20 unmodernized Mangustas as a stop-gap to serve through the early and mid-1990s. Much of the time lag in these cases was typically due to the complexity of state-of-the-art weapons systems, while the complex structures and combinations of metal and composite materials extended flight test and fatigue test programs beyond normal limits.

This slowing of pace as the frontiers of technology were pushed back inevitably left room for opportunist manufacturers to come through with less sophisticated equipment, unashamedly modified from existing types. Agusta themselves followed this path with the A 109, which had developed into a military helicopter from a civil design via police use. The Argentine Army employed the type

TV, FLIR, a laser rangefinder and direct optics sensors.

The four-nation NH90 project was intended to provide NATO with a helicopter for the nineties — hence the designation. France's Aérospatiale, Germany's MBB, Italy's Agusta and Holland's Fokker were the surviving partners, the UK having pulled out in April 1987. Deliveries were to start in 1996 — and, as might be expected with a project involving so many partners, the multirole possibilities were almost endless.

Among the intended major variants of the type were the NFH-90 (NATO Frigate Helicopter) with anti-submarine warfare and surface attack as its missions, and the TTH-90 tactical transport with search and rescue among its roles. Power was supplied by two 2100shp Rolls-Royce/Turboméca RTM 322 or similar General Electric turboshafts. The type boasted many advanced design features: a titanium main rotor hub with elastomeric bearings, composite rotor structure, a bearingless tail rotor and a quadruplex fly-by-wire system with multi-cycle blade pitch controls to minimize vibration. Reduced maintenance was assured, while an ability to operate in temperatures of plus 50 to minus 40 degrees was claimed.

In a somewhat less sophisticated vein, Sikorsky's S-76 Spirit made the crossover from the civil to the military market — like the Agusta A 109, to which it was comparable. The H-76 Eagle, as it was styled in imitation of the US service nomenclature, could boast air-to-air or air-to-surface missiles fired via a roof or mast-mounted sight. One of its more interesting features was its pilot-compensated armament pylons which, by adjusting the angle of attack in flight, added 3–4 knots to the Spirit's speed. Indeed, the type's swiftness was illustrated in 1982 when Thomas Doyle established a world speed record for a 500km closed circuit of 346km/h (215mph).

The S-76 proved the basis for an invaluable research vehicle from 1986 onwards when a

ABOVE: After a successful civil career, the twin-turbine Sikorsky S-76 was pitched at the military market, the makers even inventing an H-76 'service designation'. The pictured aircraft is being demonstrated to the Korean Army.

ABOVE: A full-size mock-up of the NH 90, a helicopter for the 1990s developed by Germany, France, Italy and Holland. Many variants of the advanced twin-engine type were planned to serve the four participating nations' air arms.

single-pilot cockpit was added to a standard S-76, this taking the form of an outgrowth at the nose. The result was Shadow (an acronym for Sikorsky Helicopter Advanced Demonstrator of Operator Workload), an attempt to evaluate how much cockpit visibility (or, indeed, lack of it) increased pilot workload. The test pilot's cockpit featured large window areas that could be partially or totally covered while the occupant's reaction was assessed, the 'normal' cockpit being occupied by a check pilot to ensure safety. Many advanced systems were installed at various times, including fly-by-wire, remote map reader, sidearm controls, a voice inter-

active system, Forward Looking Infra Red radar and head-up display, and a helmet-mounted cathode ray tube with touch-sensitive screens.

The Soviet Mil design bureau had long been famed for its huge rotorcraft, many of which had claimed the distinction in their time of being the world's largest. The Mi-12, first flown in 1968, had attained a maximum payload record of 88,635 pounds – equal to some 500 men – but had failed to reach production after encountering development problems. Then came the mighty Mi-26 Halo, rightly regarded as the world's most capable helicopter. With a rotor diameter of 105 feet

ABOVE: The prototype Sikorsky S-72, pictured in 1978. The type was used to experiment with the X-Wing concept utilizing jet propulsion and the stationary rotor blade acting as a wing.

LEFT AND RIGHT: The Mil Mi-26 Halo, holder of several world rotorcraft payload-to-height records and the first helicopter to boast an eight-blade rotor. A load of 100 infantrymen was possible.

(eight blades — the first ever to do so) its cargo hold was more akin to a fixed-wing tactical transport such as the Lockheed C-130 or Antonov An-12. Military equipment was far more likely to form the payload than the 100 combat-armed infantrymen that comprised its maximum human load.

The Mi-26 had so far only been exported to India by 1990. Eight years earlier, it had established five world helicopter payload to height records, eclipsing those set by the Sikorsky Skycrane and Mil Mi-12. The most impressive of these was set on 3 February 1982 when, piloted by G V Alfeurov, it lifted a payload of 55,115 pounds to 13,451 feet and a total mass of 125,153.8 pounds to 6560 feet. Interestingly, the massive rotor had traditional steel spars for reliability and to ensure torsional stiffness. But in other ways, including a weight-saving titanium rotor head, the Mi-26 was certainly state of the art.

The future might well belong to a hybrid helicopter such as the Sikorsky S-72, which used compressed air blasting from slits in the blades to stop the rotor in flight. The type then effectively became a fixed-wing jet with speeds of up to 361mph (582km/h). Known informally as the X-wing project, this resulted from the S-72 — originally a late seventies rotor systems research helicopter — being modified to test the idea that, after take-off as a rotary-wing aircraft, the rotor would be fixed. The 'X-wing' thus formed would permit speeds of up to 288mph, but by the late eighties the project had been becalmed by lack of funds.

Very definitely a going concern — and of great concern to NATO — was the concept of a helicopter fighter even more advanced than Mil's Mi-28. And it came from a totally unexpected source. Kamov's Hokum ground attack or air-to-air fighter helicopter represented a significant switch from the shipboard ASW types that had successfully occupied the bureau for most of its history. What *was* known at the time of writing was

ABOVE: The Bell XV-15 converts from forward to vertical flight by swiveling its wingtip-mounted power plants. The experimental type was used in the 1980s as part of the V-22 Osprey.

that Hokum first flew in 1984 and was still undergoing flight testing five years later. Its co-axial contra-rotating rotors will come as no surprise to observers of Kamov's previous products — but the swept tips for high subsonic rotor speed were a notable departure. A sophisticated sensor pack was situated under a streamlined nose — but the helicopter's *raison d'être* was already a source of contention. Veniamen Kashyanikov, the bureau's deputy chief designer, would not be drawn as to its capabilities when quizzed by observers at the Helitech '89 trade show at Redhill, Britain. Hokum had no anti-tank capability, said the US Department of Defense — they believed it to be a specialized all-weather killer armed with air-to-air missiles and a rapid-fire gun. Infrared suppressors and IR decoy dispensers were carried to ward off the unwelcome attention of surface-to-air missiles.

Hokum would give the Soviets a significant rotary-wing air superiority capability. 'The system has no current Western counterpart,' claimed the Department of Defense. Soviet military theoretician Major General M Belov went on record as saying that 'Just as tanks have always been the most effective weapon against tanks, helicopters are the most efficacious means of fighting helicopters.' If this reflects Soviet military thinking at the highest level, then the existence of Hokum should come as no surprise.

Although not strictly a helicopter, the convertiplane format was being investigated once more in the late eighties and early nineties. One such was the Bell XV-15, commissioned jointly by NASA and the US Army. Its wingtip-mounted twin rotors were too large in diameter to allow conventional take-offs and landings: these had to be achieved in helicopter form. Bell had first attempted this format of aircraft with the X-22A in 1965 — and, unlike most research machines regarded as aircraft, tilted its power plants only, rather than the whole wing. The XV-15 flew with advanced technology rotor blades in November 1987 as part of the Bell-Boeing V-22 Osprey program initiated in 1982 by the US Army but subsequently transferred to the Navy when the Army withdrew. Officially a multi-mission tilt-rotor aircraft, its V-for-vertical take-off aircraft designation suggested it was not regarded as a helicopter — and, indeed, the Navy intends to replace the fixed-wing S-3 Viking on anti-submarine duties. But a hovering capability and a short take-off range of over 200 miles made it potentially the most devastating anti-submarine weapon yet, combining fixed-wing speed and range with helicopter maneuverability.

BELOW: Sikorsky's Advanced Composite Airframe Program (ACAP) flight test aircraft pictured over the Florida Everglades. The first fully militarized composite aircraft to fly, its non-metal construction represents the likely shape of helicopters of the 21st century.

RIGHT AND BELOW: The Bell X-22 Osprey convertiplane pictured at rest and during sea trials aboard a US Navy carrier. Despite the fuselage description, the program was initiated in 1982 by the Army who later withdrew in favor of the Navy. The convertiplane format with swiveling wingtip rotors theoretically combined vertical take-off capability with a fixed wing aircraft's speed and load-carrying capacity.

Bell took another partner, McDonnell Douglas (now owners of Hughes), to attack the LHX (light helicopter experimental) program unveiled by the US Army in 1982. A single bearingless main rotor was combined with a composite construction developed from the experimental Advanced Composite Airframe Program (ACAP) flown in 1985. This was intended to show that weight savings (target 22 per cent), cost savings (17 per cent), greater survivability and a smaller radar signature could be achieved by the use of such materials. Bell and Sikorsky both competed against each other, each also completing a metal version for comparison purposes. With a ring-fan tail rotor, twin 1200 shp T800 turboshafts and the ability to fire Hellfire and Stinger missiles, the LHX would eventually serve as an armed reconnaissance light attack and air-to-air combat type, with 2100 such helicopters required.

The concept of a non-metal helicopter armed with laser-guided missiles would have seemed amazing to Heinrich Focke when he turned from building the Reich's premier fighting machines to experimenting with military rotorcraft. But he would surely approve of the fact that the helicopter, in its many shapes and forms, is now an accepted tool of modern warfare, with weapons systems every bit as complex as the airframes in which they reside.

INDEX

ACKNOWLEDGMENTS

The Publishers would like to thank Design-23, Moira Dykes for picture research and Ron Watson for the index. They would also like to thank the following agencies and institutions for the use of photographs on the pages noted below:

Aerospatiale: pages 49 right /Aviation Picture Library: 49 top /MARS: 1 below, 47 below, /TRH: 46
Austin J Brown, Aviation Picture Library: pages 1 left, 14, 17 below, 38 top, 40, 42 left, 43 top, 45 below, 52, 61 both, 63 below, 64 below, 68 top, 70 top, 71 left, 72 both, 74 both, 75 below, 76, 78 top
MJ Hooks: pages 2 below, 6, 9 both, 12 top, 15 top, 16 both, 17 top, 19 both, 20, 21 top, 23 top, 27, 30 below, 31 both, 34, 35 below, 42 right, 43 below, 45 top, 47 top, 51 below, 63 top, 68 below, 69 top
Hulton-Deutsch Collection: page 18 below
Lockheed-California Co.: page 33 top
MARS:/Augusta SPA: page 71 right /Boeing-Vertol Company, Philadelphia: page 10 below /Fairchild Republic Company, Maryland: page 10 top
MBB: page 70 below /TRH: page 49 left
Novosti Press Agency: page 26, 54, 55 top, 59 below
PhotoPress: pages 21 below, 24 below, 39, 71 top
Photri Inc, Alexandria, Virginia: pages 11 top, 13 both, 15 below, 24 top, 28, 33 below, 35 top, 53, 64 top, 65, 66, 69 below, 75 top, 78 below
Sikorsky Aircraft: pages 8, 12 below, 18 top /Aviation Picture Library: pages 58 top, 77 /TRH: pages 2 top, 52-53, 73
The Research House: pages 21 center, 23 below, 32 right, 55 below /Euromissile: page 44 /McDonnell Douglas: page 1 right /E Nevill: pages 25, 50 /John Norris: page 38 below /M Roberts: page 37 both
UPI Bettmann Newsphotos: page 30 top
US Army Photograph: page 11 below
US National Archives: pages 4-5, 32 left, 36, 42 top
US Navy Photograph: page 59 top /MARS: page 56 /TRH: pages 60, 62
Westland Helicopters: page 22 /MARS: pages 3, 48